A LITTLE BIT

OF

BUDDHA

A LITTLE BIT

OF

BUDDHA

AN INTRODUCTION TO
BUDDHIST THOUGHT

CHAD MERCREE

STERLING ETHOS
New York

STERLING ETHOS
New York

An Imprint of Sterling Publishing
1166 Avenue of the Americas
New York, NY 10036

STERLING ETHOS and the distinctive Sterling logo are registered trademarks
of Sterling Publishing Co., Inc.

ISBN 978-1-4549-1302-3

Distributed in Canada by Sterling Publishing
⅃ Canadian Manda Group, 664 Annette Street
Toronto, Ontario, Canada M6S 2C8
Distributed in the United Kingdom by GMC Distribution Services
Castle Place, 166 High Street, Lewes, East Sussex, England BN7 1XU
Distributed in Australia by Capricorn Link (Australia) Pty. Ltd.
P.O. Box 704, Windsor, NSW 2756, Australia

For information about custom editions, special sales, and premium and corporate purchases,
please contact Sterling Special Sales at 800-805-5489 or specialsales@sterlingpublishing.com.

Manufactured in the United States of America

10   9

www.sterlingpublishing.com

CONTENTS

INTRODUCTION: WHAT IS BUDDHISM?

From its humble origins in remote India to its modern expansion across the globe, Buddhism has retained its simple message of peaceful spiritual awakening and has inspired hundreds of millions of followers. Today there are well over three hundred million modern Buddhists, and millions more who are inspired by the Buddha's message. There has been a particular explosion of interest in the Western world following the exile of the Dalai Lama, leader of one of the main branches of Buddhism, from Tibet in 1959. *A Little Bit of Buddha* shares the world of Buddhists and the words of the Buddha in a clear and simple manner. Along the way you'll also learn some basic Buddhist practices to gain firsthand experiences of what Buddhism has to offer.

The heart of Buddhism blossoms from one source—the life and teachings of Siddhartha Gautama, the man we know as the Buddha. He taught a method of self-liberation and rejected the gods and goddesses of the Hindu religion of his native India. He taught his followers to look within for spiritual growth and wisdom, and offered a simple, though rigorous, path to achieve enlightenment, or transcendent wisdom. To achieve enlightenment means that you are no longer bound to come back to life over and over again, a process called reincarnation. Instead, enlightened beings transcend time and space and experience a new form of existence outside of reality as we understand it. Over the millennia, the Buddha's followers have developed myriad interpretations about exactly what the Buddha's teachings meant and how best to achieve enlightenment. Today there are several distinct Buddhist schools, and the Buddha's teachings have been incorporated into many spiritual disciplines.

Our modern world is full of external distraction. These distractions seem to proliferate day by day in the form of shiny gadgets, the race for more and more lucrative careers, or the endless repetition of the twenty-four-hour news cycle. The external world demands constant attention through increasingly insidious ways. To serious Buddhists, these are all distractions from the spiritual path and hold only fleeting pleasure. They see time as a precious commodity and spend as much time as possible developing their consciousness in preparation for enlightenment.

We all lament over how busy our lives are. Each generation yearns for the days of yesteryear, when things always seemed so much simpler. You may be surprised to learn that things were no different during the life of the Buddha, or in any era in the last 2,500 years. Whether from family duty, social upheaval, environmental change, or the pursuit of personal dreams and goals, the life of every human being is full of activity and distraction. According to Buddhists, these life experiences can be powerful tools to assist in our spiritual awakening but too often grab our attention and pull us out of the moment.

Buddhism has become an extremely complex religion, akin to all the major religions of the world. There are thousands of texts on Buddhism in dozens of languages. Many are similar and it would be impossible to collect them all in one primary text or encapsulate them in a single narrative. Instead, we will start at the beginning and look at the history and development of Buddhist thought. In Chapter 1 we'll go backward in time over 2,500 years to learn more about how Siddhartha Gautama became the Buddha and what some of his first teachings were. We'll discover what is known about the Buddha's early life and the events that shaped the foundation for his enlightenment. He was an ordinary human being who lived an extraordinary life before dying around age eighty. He experienced joy, sorrow, pleasure, pain, hope, and fear—just as we all do today. Unlike most of us, however, he discovered a method of securing complete inner peace and joy unaffected by the outside world. He came to see ordinary reality as a very intense dream, and he learned to awaken from within.

According to tradition that's perhaps peppered with a bit of myth, the twenty-nine-year-old Siddhartha experienced a series of events that catapulted him onto an intense path of spiritual awakening for six years. At its peak he achieved enlightenment, or Nirvana. He believed he perceived the true nature of reality and synthesized his beliefs into the teachings on the Four Noble Truths, the subject of Chapter 2. The Buddha began teaching what he knew and developed what he called the Middle Way, or the Noble Eightfold Path to enlightenment. In Chapter 3 we'll examine the Buddha's explanation of the Eightfold Path and its relationship to the Four Noble Truths.

Moving on from the Buddha's basic teachings, Chapter 4 explores the process of spiritual awakening from a Buddhist perspective. Buddhists have a fascinating worldview wherein we exist in one of six basic dream-realities, from the heavenly to the hellish. We'll also learn about how karma affects the way we live in this life and future lives. Buddhism is about self-development and self-awakening, an achievement that requires years of dedicated practice to achieve. During this time revelations about oneself and the nature of reality may come abruptly, only to be followed again by years of quiet practice. The sudden jumps in spiritual development can happen at the most random times. The process is unique for each of us, but the Buddha recognized four levels of enlightenment by which to gauge one's practice. The Buddha taught his disciples about the Three Jewels that can help those on the path to awakening to build a network of support and stay focused on the end goal, enlightenment. Chapter 5 explores each jewel: Buddha, Dharma, and Sangha, in more detail.

A typical first impression of Buddhism for those living in the Western world is an image of the Dalai Lama dressed in saffron robes and holding beads. He looks happy and content. Many people desire a more peaceful and contented life but aren't interested in joining a monastery and becoming a monk or a nun. Over the millennia, countless variations of Buddhism emerged, many of which are at odds with one another. Some schools of thought practiced in monasteries, while others blended into the everyday world. As in Christianity, Islam, and other megareligions, the sheer number of people involved in Buddhist philosophy led to differences in belief about what true adherents looked and acted like. At its core, however, Buddhism is a path of peace and compassion. Chapter 6 sheds light on how easy it is to practice Buddhism in the modern world.

Buddhism is about becoming your own center, about waking up to your true innate self. What does this look like? How can we hope to embrace this with so many distractions and responsibilities in our daily lives? Chapter 7 reminds us of the importance of living from our center no matter what's happening around us. In this way, the precepts of Buddhism are the same whether you are a monk in a monastery or the CEO of a large corporation. Buddhism is not a philosophy of the mind but of the heart, and the concept of *boddhichitta*, or loving-kindness, exemplifies this better than any aspect of Buddhist philosophy. Boddhichitta is a powerful expression of the Buddhist principles of love, compassion, and peacefulness, and is one of the reasons Buddhism has become so popular in the modern world. Living from our centers, from love, we naturally embody the principle of boddhichitta, loving-kindness. At the end of Chapter 7 you'll learn a brief exercise that will help you experience a glimmer of loving-kindness that Buddhists try to practice throughout their daily lives.

For Buddhists, life is a precious gift not to be wasted. Buddhists see humanity as the ideal opportunity to spiritually awaken, and serious Buddhists devote their lives to meditation and inner spiritual growth. In Chapter 8 we'll delve into Buddhists' concepts of death, time, and the ever-present now and learn how they dealt with these issues in their spiritual practices. Buddhists use every opportunity to awaken, whether in daily life, in the dreamtime, or even during the death process. Their view of death and life is fascinating, and makes up the core of Buddhist philosophy.

The techniques of the Buddhists are guides to follow as we awaken, but ultimately our own awakening will be unique and unrepeatable. No matter if our days are spent in the confines of a monastery or a cubicle, meditation goes hand in hand with mindfulness and is an important part of the Buddhist's path. Chapter 9 discusses the benefits of meditation and includes a brief meditation exercise to give you a personal experience of mindfulness.

In the modern world, few of us would choose to leave our entire existence behind for a life within the walls of a monastery. While millions of Buddhists choose to live in this way, there are millions more who devoutly follow the teachings of the Buddha in the everyday world. These people find a balance between home life, careers, and spiritual practice. Buddhist philosophy is the path of peace, and Chapter 10 shows us how easy it is to balance our spiritual and material lives. No matter how complicated life may seem, we can always do simple things to bring more peace into the world. All we need to do is remember.

Finally, we'll round out this book with a list of suggested readings for those seeking to delve deeper into the rich cultural legacy that is Buddhism.

A hallmark of the Buddha's teachings is their simple message in a complex format. Knowing one day he would die, the Buddha exhaustively explained every minute detail of achieving enlightenment. He broke down every concept into categories and subcategories. Each subcategory could be explained for hours or days. After the Buddha died, his students began discussing and analyzing his teachings even further. Over the past 2,500 years, thousands of Buddhists have written about the words of the Buddha and the practices he shared. This book merely scratches the surface of these teachings, but even so, the information can be overwhelming to newcomers. If this happens to you, set down the book and come back to it in a little while. It's a lot to take in.

Buddhism is called a religion, but it is really a philosophy of living consciously in this life in order to live forever in another life. The other life is achieved through enlightenment and is so foreign to human consciousness that it has to be experienced to be truly understood. The Buddha said a few interesting things about reality. The first is translated as follows: "Our theories of the eternal are as valuable as are those which a chick which has not broken its way through its shell might form of the outside world." In other words, we don't know anything about what's really going on. Another saying goes, "Only the experience of Nirvana makes it comprehensible to the wise." The entire focus of Buddhism is inner self-development. Generations of seasoned

Buddhists have written down their take on how to best approach self-development. These masters offer many ways and theories on the best path to enlightenment, the Buddhist's highest level of personal development. But ultimately the awakening must be achieved by each individual person. The Buddha asked his students to work out their own salvation. "Do not depend on others," he said.

Let's begin, then, with the story of Siddhartha Gautama, the ordinary man who would become the Buddha . . .

1

THE LIFE OF THE BUDDHA

THE LIFE OF SIDDHARTHA GAUTAMA IS RELA-
tively well known. It has been over 2,500 years since his
birth, however, and there are many details of his life we
will never know. Historians agree he was an actual person who lived
and died in northeastern India near modern-day Nepal around 560
BCE (before the Common Era), experienced a profound spiritual
awakening after a period of seeking, and then founded a monastic
order based on his discoveries and experiences.

As for the details provided by Buddhist literature about
Siddhartha's life, written accounts vary between Buddhist sects. A sect
is similar to a Christian denomination, and just as there are varying
accounts about the details of the life and times of Jesus, so there are
for the Buddha. However, it is commonly accepted that he was born
into a relatively wealthy family in an area called Lumbini and raised
in the town of Kapilavastu, which some archeologists believe to be

the modern village of Tilaurakot in Nepal, about six miles west of the forest of Lumbini, where he is believed to have been born.

Beyond this there is little confirmed fact. It is said that shortly after his birth a wise man named Asita visited Siddhartha's father, King Suddhodana. The wise man told the king that his newborn son, Prince Siddhartha, had two possible destinies: He would either become a great king or a wise holy man. The boy's life direction would be determined by one simple thing—whether or not young Siddhartha was ever allowed to see life beyond the palace walls. If Siddhartha left the palace he would become a holy man; if not, he would become king. Not surprisingly, King Suddhodana decided to make a king out of his son and did everything in his power to prevent Siddhartha from going outside. Other variations of the story exist but this one is the most common.

Siddhartha's confined life continued for twenty-nine years. Siddhartha enjoyed the best things in life. He ate the best food, enjoyed the finest entertainments and companionship, and wanted for nothing. Siddhartha wished to please his father the king, even though he had a nagging feeling that something was off. Siddhartha eventually married and, according to some versions, had at least one child. He also became a skilled warrior and tried his best to take part in all the things his father suggested he do. All of Siddhartha's activities, however, took place within the palace walls.

Still, the desire to see life outside the palace grew stronger and stronger each year. As his father always refused or found new ways to distract Siddhartha from going outside, Siddhartha arranged a trip beyond the palace with his charioteer Channa. Again, accounts vary, and some stories say that the king finally relented and secretly prepared a special route for Siddhartha to travel filled with fine things and healthy, happy subjects. Either way, Siddhartha went forth and explored beyond the walls of the palace with Channa.

Siddhartha experienced four sights along his journey, or some say along four different journeys, beyond the palace walls. The first thing he beheld was an old man. Now this was quite a shock to Siddhartha, as he'd never seen such a person inside the palace; Siddhartha's father kept such things hidden from his son. Siddhartha asked Channa what kind of person they were looking at and Channa replied that it was an old man, and that aging happens to everything alive. Siddhartha suddenly realized that everyone he knew, including his wife, would one day grow old and weak.

Continuing on their journey, Siddhartha saw a sick person on the side of road. Siddhartha had never seen disease or sickness within the palace, either, as his father kept this hidden from his son as well. Siddhartha was just as surprised by disease as he was by aging. He asked Channa what was going on. Channa explained that everyone is susceptible to disease and sickness. Siddhartha desired to help the sick man, but Channa prevented him, saying the sick man had the plague, which was contagious. This troubled Siddhartha, but they continued on their journey.

Farther along the road they beheld the most shocking sight yet for young Siddhartha, that of a dead body. Some accounts say Siddhartha watched the dead body be carried to a pyre and set on fire. Either way, the sight of the dead person troubled Siddhartha, and he again asked Channa to explain what was going on. Channa revealed that death happens to every living thing; there is no escape and nothing can prevent it. According to some accounts, upon hearing Channa's words Siddhartha decided to find a way to prevent death.

It's not hard to imagine Siddhartha's distress at suddenly realizing the reality of pain and suffering in the world. Siddhartha's first exploration beyond the palace walls was a life-changing experience. He was lost in thought about what he'd seen when Channa drove the chariot by an ascetic monk. Though dressed in rags and bone-thin, the man was smiling and apparently content. They stopped the chariot and Siddhartha asked about the man. Channa explained that this was a holy man who begged for food in exchange for teaching people how to be peaceful and good. In the face of everything he'd just seen, Siddhartha wondered how the holy man could seem so happy. He and Channa returned to the palace where Siddhartha reflected on the day's events. He decided to become a monk to learn how to be happy again.

Soon after the chariot ride, Siddhartha received news that his wife had given birth to a son. Instead of feeling happy, however, he felt depressed. He had brought another being into the world of suffering, but also now he could never leave the palace to become a monk. In a moment of truly depressive storytelling, one version of the Buddha's life goes so far as to say he named his son Rahula, which means "Obstacle." Poor kid.

As Siddhartha approached thirty, with a growing family and an assured title of king in his future, he turned his back on everything he knew. He gave it all up and left the palace and his family and friends to seek out holy men. He was determined to learn about old age, pain and suffering, and death. For the next six years Siddhartha was a spiritual seeker. At first he studied with more well-known teachers of his day. He mastered meditation and other practices. At one point Siddhartha decided the best way for him to understand pain and suffering was to live as an extreme ascetic, a person who endured all manner of deliberate hardship in order to transcend their own attachment to suffering. Practices included prolonged fasting or self-starvation, self-cutting and other forms of body mutilation, prolonged holding of the breath, and other drastic measures.

After a lengthy period as an ascetic, Siddhartha was still unable to transcend pain and suffering. The story goes that at the moment he realized the path of the extreme ascetic was no good, a young woman happened by, offering Siddhartha milk and rice. He accepted her kind gesture and decided enough was enough. In a nutshell, Siddhartha decided to tone things down and practice *anapanasati*, what we would today call "mindfulness meditation," a type of meditation that follows the breath through the body while at the same time developing a great awareness of the body in general. This method marked the beginning of Siddhartha's final stage of meditations before he experienced a state of enlightenment. Buddhists see mindfulness meditation as a means of reaching Nirvana, or enlightenment, discussed later on in this book.

Finding success with deep peaceful meditation, at the age of thirty-five Siddhartha decided to sit beneath a fig tree until he reached enlightenment. This is said to have occurred near the town of Bodh Gaya in India, and today the type of fig tree under which Siddhartha performed his final meditations before enlightenment is known as the Bodhi tree. He sat for days under the Bodhi tree in meditation without stopping. At last he broke through the limitations of his mind and experienced enlightenment. He stopped meditating and decided to teach others what he had discovered. From this point on he became known as the Buddha, which means "awakened one."

No one knows for sure, but the Buddha died at around eighty years old, dying around 480 BCE in the town of Kushinagar, India. There are several versions of exactly how he died, but most revolve around him becoming sick or poisoned by food. Post-enlightenment, he attracted a large following, started a monastic order, or Sangha, and transmitted his wisdom via word of mouth, the Dharma. There are thousands of lines of text that record the many teachings Buddha delivered to his students. His words have been translated into myriad languages and scholars have interpreted and reinterpreted his teachings almost from the moment he died.

The oldest surviving Buddhist texts come from northwestern Pakistan and were written in the first century BCE. They are known as the Gandhari texts. During the gap of over three hundred years between Siddhartha's life and the writing of the Gandharis, several variations of Buddhism arose. Many of these variations, or sects, differ on certain points and have led to the creation of several schools of Buddhism. This trend continued throughout the centuries, with perhaps thousands of various schools and movements expressing their own interpretation of the Buddha's teachings over the last two thousand years. There are too many to name in this book, and while many sects have faded into obscurity with time, there are many alive and well today, and as our understanding of Buddhism continues to grow, so does our interpretation of what the Buddha taught.

Scholars lump all Buddhist schools into several categories. East Asian Buddhism includes China, Japan, Korea, Singapore, and Vietnam. Mahayana or "Great Vehicle" Buddhism usually includes the teachings of the Vajrayana school as well. Theravada Buddhism includes Buddhist schools from Bangladesh, Burma, Cambodia, China, India, Laos, Malaysia, Sri Lanka, Thailand, and Vietnam. Tibetan Buddhism covers Buddhists from Bhutan, Mongolia, and Tibet, as well as certain parts of China, India, and Russia. Other forms of Buddhism not included above are Newar and Nyingma from Tibet and the Tangmi esoteric tradition found throughout Southeast Asia. Many of these schools are a combination of traditional folk beliefs and other religions blended into standard Buddhist thought.

At times, the history of Buddhism becomes a tangled mess, and there is a lot of history left to be rediscovered. As Buddhism spread over the globe, people added their own cultural and religious flavors to the Buddha's original teachings. In this book we'll focus on the traditional views held by the Buddha, as there are several basic features of Buddhism that the majority of Buddhist sects share. The first traditional teaching of the Buddha deals with the Buddha's experience riding through town with Channa, the charioteer, and is the basis for Chapter 2.

2

THE FOUR NOBLE TRUTHS

ONCE SIDDHARTHA GAUTAMA ACHIEVED A state of enlightenment, he was called the Buddha, the awakened one. He was a young man of thirty-five and decided to spend the rest of his life teaching others what he had discovered. He soon attracted a band of followers who also wished to achieve the enlightened state of Nirvana.

It is said that the first of Buddha's teachings, his first sermon, centered on the Four Noble Truths. These truths are the result of Buddha's experience riding beyond the palace walls with his charioteer Channa. The four truths all deal with the nature of *dukkha*, which literally translates as "dissatisfaction" but is commonly called "suffering." Other meanings include stress, emptiness, or an inability to feel good on a permanent basis. For the Buddha, his nagging feelings of dissatisfaction about his existence, even while trapped within the palace walls, were an indication of his readiness for spiritual training.

The Four Noble Truths go as follows:

- The truth of dukkha.

- The truth of the origin of dukkha.

- The truth of the end of dukkha.

- The truth of the path leading to the end of dukkha.

Let's explore the meaning behind these very similar phrases. These four short sentences comprise the foundation of Buddhist thought and teaching.

THE FIRST TRUTH: DISSATISFACTION

The first noble truth says that dissatisfaction is a part of daily life. It is inevitable. From a Buddhist's perspective, every experience is transitory. Any feelings of happiness or joy arise, are experienced, and then inevitably fade away to be replaced by the next feeling or experience. The Buddha observed that positive experiences are always interspersed with negative experiences of pain and suffering, sorrow and anxiety, stress and fear. The word *dukkha* means all of these things, and it acknowledges change as a constant in the universe. To help his students understand the gravity of *dukkha*, the Buddha broke it down into three aspects: *dukkha-dukkha*, *viparinama-dukkha*, and *sankhara-dukkha*.

SUFFERING: Dukkha-dukkha is what we would commonly think of as suffering, and it includes emotional and physical pain. Its cause could be physical or psychological.

CHANGE: Viparinama-dukkha means dissatisfaction caused by the experience of change in our lives, such as the ending of a positive experience. In other words, we are attached to things not changing and are dissatisfied as a result because everything changes. So this dukkha relates to attachment to psychological points of view.

BEINGNESS: Sankhara-dukkha means dissatisfaction because we exist, or the suffering of individuality. This also indicates dissatisfaction with the stages of life, as in the cliché of those who relive peak high school experiences, are never satisfied with their current situation and look forward to a happier future, or find fault with the many ways their current lives are not as perfect as they'd like them to be.

This last point may seem odd, but to Buddhists, the entire universe is samsara, an illusion, a transitory state of being within which we are in a sense trapped. A dream. The goal, then, of a Buddhist is to "wake up" from the world into which we're born. Simply existing in this world comes with it a great opportunity to awaken to our true natures. In contrast to the true spiritual self, humans experience a false sense of self created by the external world of illusion in which we live. This sense of self is based on many factors, but the Buddha broke these factors down into what he called the Five Aggregates.

The Five Aggregates

To further explain sankhara-dukkha, Buddhists see individuality as an illusion created by the Five Skandhas or "Aggregates." These aggregates combine to form a false sense of the self, or sankhara-dukkha.

The Five Aggregates are as follows:

THE AGGREGATE OF MATTER

Matter means the physical world around us, and it is formed by four elements: earth, water, fire, and air. When the four combine in various ways, the result is our rich sensory experiences, including eyes and sight, ears and sounds, nose and smells, tongue and tastes, and touch and textures. Sometimes the mind and objects of mental creation are included in this list.

THE AGGREGATE OF SENSATION

Sensation refers to the quality of the experience of the senses derived from matter. They are listed as pleasant, unpleasant, and indifferent. A common active meditation practice is to nonjudgmentally observe how we experience the sensations of being alive.

THE AGGREGATE OF PERCEPTION

Perception means sensing in a moment in time. Becoming aware of our perceptions helps us remain in the moment and learn about the process our body, emotions, and mind go through as we respond to our environment. Understanding the aggregate of perception also helps us learn how we identify the world we live in.

THE AGGREGATE OF MENTAL FORMATION

Mental formation means all the habits we've accumulated in our lifetime that cause us to unconsciously respond to circumstances in a particular way. Mental formation can also be described as the result of the way we've experienced similar situations in the past.

THE AGGREGATE OF CONSCIOUSNESS

The last aggregate, or *skandha*, reminds us that simple physical contact or mechanical biological processes are not enough to create a response to the physical world, whether conscious or unconscious. Consciousness of some form is required to create an awareness and interpretation of a physical, emotional, or mental experience. To the Buddha, while the world may be an illusion, consciousness is real. As the goal of Buddhist philosophy is to spiritually awaken from within and perceive true reality, consciousness holds great value. It is only by making deliberate and sustained efforts to increase awareness, or consciousness, that we can hope to awaken.

I realize we're jumping in pretty deep right from the beginning, but it's important to understand the philosophy of the Buddha if we're to understand the core belief systems of Buddhists, their desire for peace, their serious attitude toward meditation, and their cultivation of compassion and joy. Buddhists believe that the Five Aggregates combine to form consciousness. But it's a consciousness that exists in an illusory world. So this means Buddhists believe our human experience is ultimately a false one: Our sense of individuality is false, the "this" and "that" of life, all sense of separation and physical space, even time itself are all illusions. Basically, until these five elements "aggregate" together, similarly as water, lime, and rock combine to form cement, there can be no consciousness. Buddha taught the concept of anatman, or "no-self." We are the result of five elements: form, sense, perception, thought forms, and, finally, consciousness. Consciousness cannot arise without the appropriate balance of the first four elements, or aggregates. While the first aggregate refers to our physical bodies, the remaining four relate to our ability to perceive, to our consciousness and psychology.

What does all of this have to do with dukkha, our inner sense of dissatisfaction with life? Buddha recognized that we are born into a world of change, live in changing bodies, and can do nothing about the laws of the physical universe. Change is a constant. Everything is in motion. This essence of change is woven into our very cells and therefore allows us no permanent sense of joy. Since we cannot rely on the physical world for joy, it is a source of dukkha, of dissatisfaction.

THE SECOND TRUTH: THE CAUSE OF SUFFERING

So if we're stuck in a state of dissatisfaction, how did we get here? The answer, according to Buddhists, is found in the second noble truth. The second noble truth says that the cause of dukkha can be known, and the cause is desire blurred by ignorance. The words used are *tanha*, or "craving," "thirst," and *avijja*, "ignorance." Craving and thirst indicate desire or grasping for something currently out of reach. So basically Buddha said that suffering is caused by desiring the wrong things out of ignorance.

There are three types of tanha, or craving. *Kama-tanha* is craving sensory pleasures and includes everything from eating a great meal to watching the perfect sunset to lovemaking. *Bhava-tanha* is craving to be important, and it relates to the ego. The desire for power, prestige, and fame, to leave a lasting mark on the world, to live forever—these are all aspects of bhava-tanha. In contrast, the final craving is *vibhava-tanha*, the desire to no longer exist, to experience nothing and pull away from life. It also can mean the desire to avoid any negativity, emotional trauma, or physical pain.

THE THIRD TRUTH: THE END OF SUFFERING

Whereas many religions pit good versus evil as the cause of human suffering, the Buddha had no such view. Suffering was an inner condition, caused in part by the way we come into being in this world but even more by the nature of desire. Without proper training we can't help but be ignorant and perpetuate our own dissatisfaction with life. Some see this worldview as very pessimistic, but to Buddhists it is neither optimistic nor pessimistic; dukkha is simply an observation of the way things are. The Four Noble Truths end on a higher note, however. The third noble truth states that it is possible to overcome all dissatisfaction.

Reaching a point of consciousness beyond dissatisfaction, pain, and suffering is an important aspect of Buddhist tradition. We achieve this transcendent state through meditation, awareness, understanding, and detachment. In many respects the process of waking up and becoming enlightened occurs when self-awareness is developed to the point where we can remain fully present in each and every moment (awareness). We are not moved to act or react by any external force (detachment) but are instead driven only by the center point of our consciousness (understanding). This center exists in a place harmonious with joy and compassion, and it is not possible to achieve enlightenment without them.

Being present all the time to every experience may seem impossible, but there are Buddhists from every generation who are said to have achieved such a state of being. The state is often described as one of detachment, but it is more correct to describe it as loving detachment, sometimes called loving-kindness. This is not the Western idea of detachment as being uncaring or aloof. The fourth noble truth outlines the recommended path to raise our consciousness to this state of being. The fourth noble truth is called the Eightfold Path of enlightenment and is covered in the following chapter.

The Buddha refined his teaching of the Four Noble Truths throughout his life and considered their understanding as essential. He said the Four Noble Truths is the core teaching and that all other teachings fit within their framework.

Living in a reality that is constantly changing inspired the Buddha to find a source of constancy. He found this in the mind. To the Buddha the mind was far more important than the body. Both have their place but one must be in charge. Most people are buffeted around by life, pushed here or there by random experiences and their reactions to those experiences. Some experiences bring joy, others sorrow. Experiences repeat endlessly from the moment of birth until death. The Buddha sought a way beyond being affected by life. The Four Noble Truths represent his solution to this problem.

Despite the doom-and-gloom approach to reality, the Buddha felt that joy and compassion were essential components on the path to enlightenment. The Buddha's perception of the mind was very different from the Western view of the mind, which is seen as divorced from emotion or caring.

There is a misperception that Buddhists embrace an aloof state of being, and that detachment means not caring. It's perhaps easier for the Western mind to perceive the teachings in this way because in our culture those who are overly mental are seen as dispassionate and uncaring.

The Buddha did not teach this. The path to enlightenment embraces a deep and profound joy and a true sense of compassion and caring for all living things while at the same time remaining detached from the samsara, or illusory reality, that constantly unfolds before our eyes. At first this may seem a difficult concept for us, but it is an integral part of the Buddhist view of reality. It is something that many Buddhists have experienced, and perhaps the best way to understand this "Buddha mind" is to experience it firsthand. A key practice in Buddhism is meditation, and those who meditate on a regular basis find peace and relaxation are key benefits of the practice.

Now let's explore in more depth the fourth noble truth, known as the Noble Eightfold Path.

3

THE NOBLE EIGHTFOLD PATH

AS WITH THE BUDDHA'S TEACHING OF THE FOUR Noble Truths, the Noble Eightfold Path contains few words but can take a lifetime to master. The Buddha considered all steps on the path to be interconnected like the spokes of a wheel. They are not step-by-step directions; a practitioner may start anywhere and gradually incorporate them all over time. In fact, the image of a spoked wheel, known as the Dharma wheel, is often used to symbolize the equal importance of each aspect of the Eightfold Path. In Buddhist tradition, it often represents the Buddha's teachings.

The Eightfold Path describes eight activities we all must do to develop our awareness in preparation for enlightenment. The spokes of the Eightfold Path are often written as right view, right intention, right speech, right action, right livelihood, right effort, right mindfulness, and right concentration, but the word "right" implies right and wrong and can lead to negative associations for those learning about them through the lens of Western culture. The word normally translated to "right" is *samyak*, which in Sanskrit is a more nuanced term that means "right, well, correct, or proper." So, no matter what direction a student chooses, the eight steps or spokes all lead to the same central state of being. All eight spokes help one another become stronger. Therefore, most schools of Buddhist thought believe it doesn't matter where a student begins the journey. Cultivating kind speech helps foster a healthy view of the world, which helps reinforce the intention to continue on the spiritual path, which helps improve meditation. In the beginning of your practice, success may be fleeting and one or another spoke of the Eightfold Path may appear to represent an easier journey depending on your mood or the day of the week. With time, the process becomes more fluid, and life is slowly transformed.

The most important aspect of a Buddhist's life is practice. It is important to practice the Eightfold Path every day during every activity. Have proper mindfulness at work, use proper speech at home, and take proper action at all times. In the beginning we are limited by our ability to remember the eight steps and provide enough concentration on our waking moments to actualize them. The process of finding success on the Eightfold Path is no different from any other task we may undertake. At first things are difficult. Our life is full of habits and preexisting patterns. Time passes and we may feel discouraged. Even so, it is important to keep practicing. Success will come.

The Four Noble Truths and the Noble Eightfold Path are the foundations of all Buddhist tradition. Mastering these core practices and understanding their meaning is a fundamental requirement of all Buddhists. Everything else you will read about Buddhism derives from the Buddha's original teachings on the Four Noble Truths and the Eightfold Path. Let's look in more depth at the Noble Eightfold Path and how to apply its principles to our daily lives.

PRAJNA, OR WISDOM

Prajna combines the first two spokes of the Eightfold Path. It is regarded as a purifying wisdom and consists of seeing reality for what it really is, a necessity for those seeking enlightenment.

Proper View

Proper view means seeing reality for what it is and looking beyond the superficial. Proper view also implies a willingness to see things as they are, because many people would rather turn a blind eye than comprehend the gravity of our human condition. The Buddha said, "There are only two mistakes one can make along the road to truth: Not pursuing the path all the way, and not beginning." Buddhists recognize the special opportunity humanity offers to those seeking enlightenment. According to the Buddha, humanity is the only form of life capable of enlightenment.

Right view also means minding our own business, focusing on our own path instead of comparison with others. The Buddha said, "Do not overrate what you have received, nor envy others. He who envies others does not obtain peace of mind." Cultivating right view helps us develop compassion for ourselves and all life, as right view implies having an understanding of the inherent emptiness of all form. Since we live in a world of form, we live in a world of emptiness. Again, Buddhists do not see these views as negative or depressing. Instead they are observations of the nature of reality. To live properly in this reality, therefore, we must accept the situation as it is and not ignore reality in order to believe this world is real and everlasting. To Buddhists, all we know is temporary, like a dream from which we must one day awaken. Proper view embraces this truth.

Proper Intention

Proper intention means consciously choosing the spiritual path toward enlightenment. The Buddha said, "All that we are is the result of what we have thought: It is founded on our thoughts, it is made up of our thoughts. If a man speaks or acts with an evil thought, pain follows him, as the wheel follows the foot of the ox that draws the carriage. All that we are is the result of what we have thought: It is founded on our thoughts, it is made up of our thoughts. If a man speaks or acts with a pure thought, happiness follows him, like a shadow that never leaves him." This concept is familiar to many of us. Pop psychology often reminds us that "you are what you think." Right intention speaks to the need to choose carefully and to be ever mindful of what we ask for, consciously and unconsciously, for that is what will happen. Intention is seen as the driver of karma, or future life situations.

Proper intention for Buddhists means cultivating the intentions of renunciation, good will, and harmlessness. These three intentions are set to counteract our unconscious thoughts, which cultivate desire, ill will, and harmfulness. To intend renunciation doesn't mean to give up all possessions, but rather to give up our attachment to them. The Buddha described our temporary existence as "a flash of lightning in a summer cloud," something ephemeral. To try to hold on to the temporary only causes dissatisfaction, or dukkha.

The purest proper intention is to seek enlightenment for the benefit of all life.

SILA, OR MORALITY

The next three spokes of the Eightfold Path are collectively called *sila*. Sila is the concept of an ultimate, perfect morality. There are many suggestions found in Buddhist writing about how to embrace sila and live a moral life. However, since Buddhism is ultimately a religion of self-development, it is up to the individual to embrace and cultivate a high morality. Morality leads to calmness and therefore assists in developing deep concentration. Advanced Buddhists no longer rely on written codes of conduct but instead are awakened enough to follow their bliss, their dharma, from a place of wisdom and compassion. Sila is composed of proper speech, action, and livelihood. In Buddhism the quality of a person's morality is seen as an indicator of that individual's experience of karma, to be discussed in the next chapter.

Proper Speech

Proper speech seems simple enough. It asks us to speak only from kindness and compassion, to say things that promote a more peaceful world. To Buddhists, speech and action are closely connected, and most Buddhists consider them to be different aspects of the same force. Speech arises from our thoughts, and so Buddhists are asked not only to say kind words but also to think them. To be full of hateful or petty thoughts, even if we never utter an unkind word, is seen as a serious impediment on the path of enlightenment. However, thought, speech, and deed work together, so if you wish to cultivate kind thoughts, then begin with kind words and deeds. Eventually the mind will follow.

Buddhists are asked to cultivate proper speech in four ways: Never tell lies. Never slander anyone for any reason. Never use rude or foul language. Never engage in gossip or mindless chatter. As mentioned above with sila, rules are set for beginning Buddhists. Advanced Buddhists reach a point where their hearts are so filled with compassion and wisdom that proper speech is a matter of course.

Proper Action

The Buddha said, "However many holy words you read, however many you speak, what good will they do you if you do not act upon them?" He also said, "No one saves us but ourselves. No one can and no one may. We ourselves must walk the path."

While proper action is often used to inspire environmental or social activism, this concept means to act in accordance with the teachings of the Buddha. It means to act mindfully, or with full awareness, with compassion and joy but with no attachment to the outcome of the action. Every effort is made to do a thing correctly and to the best of our ability; however, detachment in this sense doesn't indicate a lack of caring.

There are five commonly held things Buddhists must do to engage in proper action: Respect life, be generous, practice harmless sexuality, engage in loving speech, and cultivate good health. Sometimes these are listed in terms of what not to do (no killing, no stealing, etc.), and there is debate about exactly how far to take these statements. For example, some Buddhists are vegetarian, while others eat meat. Even early Buddhists were advised to never refuse food that was offered to them, including meat. As with proper speech, the precepts of proper action serve as guides for beginning Buddhists, while advanced Buddhists are considered to have developed wisdom and compassion to understand exactly what they are doing and therefore act appropriately.

Proper Livelihood

The five precepts of proper action apply to proper livelihood, too. Buddhists choose livelihoods, or careers, that cause no harm to other beings, though they seem to generally only include humans and animals in this mind-set. The Buddha described proper livelihood in the following way: "A [nonmonk Buddhist] should not engage in five types of business. Which five? Business in weapons, business in human beings, business in meat, business in intoxicants, and business in poison."

Proper livelihood can be a career that benefits the world in some way, or at least brings no additional harm to it. But it also means choosing life opportunities that keep the body and mind healthy and strong. The Buddha said, "To keep the body in good health is a duty; otherwise we shall not be able to keep our mind strong and clear." The Buddha was no couch potato. Alert meditation, breathing exercises, and many of the other Buddhist practices require effort. Therefore, Buddhists must choose only those activities that enhance their spiritual journey. To acquire a job that has zero negative impact in the world is quite literally impossible. At the very least a portion of nature was most likely destroyed to create the building in which you work. Proper livelihood, therefore, is to choose an honest pursuit that can be done to the best of your ability while remaining unattached to it.

SAMADHI, OR CONCENTRATION

The final spokes of the Eightfold Path are called *samadhi*. Samadhi means "to bring together," which, in terms of Buddhist philosophy, means the bringing together of the mind, or concentration. Specifically, the three spokes grouped under samadhi help develop single-pointed concentration. Through the combination of proper effort, mindfulness, and meditation, Buddhists are able to focus their attention on a single thing to such an extent they lose the sense of "selfness" that is a signature of our waking consciousness. *I am this, you are that*. With deep concentration, all separation disappears and we experience oneness.

A result of developing the ability to concentrate is the appearance of jhanas, or dhyana. Jhana means to meditate deeply. So the jhanas describe ever-deeper states of meditation that Buddhists can achieve, each one associated with special psychic abilities. Jhanas will be discussed later in Chapter 9.

Many Buddhists believe that the correct application of proper effort, mindfulness, and meditation or concentration can lead them to experience the highest levels of jhana, which are precursors to enlightenment.

Proper Effort

Proper effort means doing things to become a more generous, wise, and kind person. Effort in this case can be applied to physical tasks or mental study and comprehension, or to devoting time to a cause, helping out those in need, or doing other similar activities.

Proper effort implies knowing what it is you're working toward, as well as the best ways to get there. It doesn't mean developing an unbalanced approach to spiritual effort by becoming a workaholic or merely thinking about the ideas of enlightenment but doing nothing to cultivate them in one's own life. The Buddha said, "It is better to conquer yourself than to win a thousand battles. Then the victory is yours and cannot be taken from you."

Joy is an important part of proper effort. If there is no joy in a task or it is done merely for the sake of completion, then proper effort has not been achieved. Proper effort naturally results in feelings of joy, which is an important feeling to cultivate on the Buddhist path. The Buddha had much to say about proper efforts, such as being consistent and diligent and persevering through trying times. Proper effort means preventing or abandoning unwholesome states of being and cultivating or maintaining wholesome states of being. There are five hindrances to proper effort: sensual desire, ill will, dullness and drowsiness, restlessness and worry, and doubt.

Proper Mindfulness

Proper mindfulness means staying aware and in the present moment. To live with proper mindfulness means not worrying about the future or pining for the past. Staying present allows Buddhists to fully develop single-pointed concentration. If thoughts are scattered to the future, to the past, to other people's lives, to the five hindrances listed above, or to anything other than the present moment, then the mind cannot fully concentrate, cannot be "here." Buddhists develop awareness of their body, feelings, thoughts, and sense perceptions to help foster presence.

Cultivating a strong presence of mind is seen as important to Buddhists because enlightenment must be experienced from within. It is not a boon from a god or the gods. It is not bestowed upon Buddhists by the Buddha. Enlightenment results from efforts made by an individual. It is the consequence of a step-by-step process to fully comprehend the human condition and rise above the illusory world of duality and ignorance.

For Buddhists the mind is not the same as thought or logical deduction. Buddhists do not think about the nature of reality, suddenly realize the answer, and become enlightened. Instead, over time, the mind can be prepared to experience the nature of reality, which is an experience beyond thought or feeling. We practice the activities necessary to live the Eightfold Path, preparing ourselves through our own efforts to have greater and greater experiences of true reality.

Self-observation is one way to achieve proper mindfulness. Buddhists observe their entire natures, from breathing to thoughts and bodily sensations. Buddhists approach this practice without attachment or judgment. The goal is to simply observe what is happening and stay in the present moment.

PROPER MEDITATION

All eight principles of the Eightfold Path work in harmony to lead toward inner human perfection. Buddhists may begin anywhere they choose, but proper meditation, or proper concentration, is often seen as a culmination of the seven previous principles. It is recognized as such because Buddhists believe that through intense concentration they will be able to fully realize a state of oneness or nonduality. From this perspective, proper meditation is the aspect of the Eightfold Path that leads to the final preparatory steps before the experience of enlightenment. The goal of Buddhism is to wake up from within and perceive reality as it truly is—to awaken from samsara, the world of illusion within which we are trapped.

All serious Buddhists meditate, but there are many forms of meditation. The type that Buddhists practice is active meditation. Instead of emptying the mind for its own sake, Buddhists cultivate their mental faculties to a point of extreme concentration. They achieve this by focusing on one thing for extended periods. Their single-pointed concentration can be on the breath, a mental image such as a symbol, or an external object. Meditation may also be used to focus on a particular concept; for example, on the nature of illusion.

To achieve good concentration means overcoming the five hindrances mentioned previously: sensual desire, bad will, laziness, restlessness, and worry and doubt. Once the five hindrances have been overcome, a Buddhist is able to achieve the deeper meaning of proper meditation and experience the early stages of enlightenment.

Exercise: Mindfulness Meditation

The Buddha spoke of mindfulness meditation as the way to spiritual awakening. Mindfulness meditation is a self-observation practice. Buddha said if you can maintain a state of complete self-observation for even seven days, you will achieve enlightenment. Remaining fully present in the moment at all times is very difficult. To engage in mental commentary or emotional responses to your observations is a sign that you are no longer in the moment but are instead dwelling in the past and reflecting upon what has just been witnessed. In the eternal now, there is only awareness—there is no need for reflection upon the experience.

For those who find it difficult to remain in the present moment while the wildness and randomness of our being unfolds before our eyes, it may be helpful to practice basic mindfulness to start training the mind to concentrate. The practice is very simple and can be done anywhere. While meditating, eating, resting, driving, working, or watching TV, remain ever mindful of the endless cycle of inhalations and exhalations made by the body. The Buddha said, "Mindfulness of in-and-out breathing, when developed and pursued, is of great fruit, of great benefit. Mindfulness of in-and-out breathing, when developed and pursued, brings clear knowing and release to their culmination."

The ultimate goal of proper meditation, in the meaning of the Noble Eightfold Path, is to fully understand the Buddha's teachings.

⇥ 4 ⇤
THE PROCESS
OF AWAKENING

B UDDHISM IS THE PROCESS OF AWAKENING AND
being present to ultimate reality. This is enlightenment.
Buddhists believe that inside each human is the seed of a
bodhisattva, which means "awakened being." Eventually all beings
will awaken, and Buddhists believe the human form is best suited to
accomplishing this goal. Buddhists also believe enlightenment can be
achieved in a single lifetime with proper effort. The Buddha recognized four levels of enlightenment and called those who attained any
of the four levels noble persons. But before we look at the enlightenments, let's look at Buddhist views on reincarnation.

First of all, Buddhists do not believe we have a soul in the
Western sense of the word. They believe that our personalities—
in other words, who we are—are based on the interactions of the
Five Aggregates mentioned earlier and are greatly affected by the
twelve foundations of mind mentioned later on in Chapter 9. There

is the potential for continuity of consciousness between lives, which is strictly based upon past meditative achievements, though this is a rare occurrence. The idea of learning how to become detached from everyday existence relates to the view that very little of what we experience truly represents who we really are. Instead of a soul, there is mind awareness of greater or lesser degree. With great effort, Buddha mind awakens, allowing us to experience awareness beyond thought and emotion.

REINCARNATION AND THE SIX REALMS

Buddhists, like many Asian and Old World religions, believe in reincarnation. Reincarnation is the process of being born over and over in different bodies. In relation to the cycle of birth and death, Buddhists believe that our consciousness dictates where we are born. There are three possible states of existence we can be born into, in three different realms: formless, form, and desire. The first two realms are for more spiritually advanced beings. In terms of the human condition, we exist in the desire realm. Within the desire realm are six possible states of being, or six realms.

The six realms of existence are hell, hungry ghosts, animals, humans, demigods, and gods. All humans can see at least the realm of animals. The realms are not specific planets or anything temporal; they are states of awareness within which all life, as pure consciousness, is stuck in a repetitive dream state.

Hell

Naraka is the realm of hell. It is the lowest level of consciousness, filled with all forms of anger and hatred. It is a world of violence and intense pain and suffering.

Hungry Ghosts

Preta is the realm of the hungry ghosts. Beings are born into this realm that cultivated strong possessiveness and desire in previous lives. It is full of a life-form called hungry ghosts because these beings are always hungry and thirsty for experience and are never satisfied.

Animals

Tiryag-yoni is the realm of animals. In the Buddhist view, animals are all very stupid and self-centered. While they may demonstrate behaviors that indicate a capacity for caring, they also show great prejudice toward other beings and care only for their own kind.

Humans

Manusya is the realm of humans. Buddhists believe this the luckiest place to incarnate because it's the only one in which enlightenment is possible. They believe that the special qualities that result in a human being, the Five Aggregates described earlier, are unique among living beings. Buddhists also believe that most people waste this precious opportunity by cultivating an overly materialistic or petty life and wind up reincarnating in one of the other lower realms after death. Few people live honorably enough to merit another human life.

Demigods

Asura is the realm of the demigods. You know the saying, "The road to hell is paved with good intentions"? Well, that may well describe this place. This realm is for those who tried to do good deeds in a previous life but still manifested rationalization, deception, envy, jealousy, or other falsity and brought harm to others. In Buddhist tradition, the beings that live in Asura have an easier life than humans do but are plagued by jealousy because, just as animals can see humans, the beings of Asura can perceive the realm of the gods, the next realm of existence. And this drives Asurans mad with envy.

Gods

Deva is the realm of the gods. The realm of devas is filled with bliss and every comfort one could imagine. It is a spiritually refined realm, though still as much a part of illusory samsara as our world. Inhabitants of the devic realm are at a supreme disadvantage, however, according to Buddhists. Life is so good here that there is no "call to action," no sense of dukkha or dissatisfaction. With no life friction to move them, these beings use up all of their good karma built up from previous lives simply lounging in paradise. Although they are very long lived compared with humans, they do eventually die and are usually reborn into a lower state of consciousness in a lower realm.

It may also be apparent that the emotional states described in the various realms can all be found in the human realm. There are humans full of anger and rage who experience a hellish life, humans who have little interest in mental development but focus only on the body like an animal, people who are never satisfied, like those who live in the realm of the hungry ghosts, those who are always frustrated by success that seems just out of reach no matter how hard they try, and those who are born into luxury and live like gods and goddesses and amount to nothing in life. In fact, there are schools of Buddhism that believe that all humans experience every realm of existence during their human spiritual path to enlightenment. In Zen Buddhism it is expected that Buddhists will go through these stages during the practice of *zazen*, a type of meditation. At the end of this grueling process, the practitioner is said to be free from suffering and has transcended dukkha.

FOUR TYPES OF ENLIGHTENMENT

If someone has been lucky enough to merit a human life and spent many lives making conscious efforts to further awaken from within by following the Eightfold Path, then maybe, just maybe, he or she will advance enough in a single lifetime to experience the beginning stages of enlightenment. Otherwise, via reincarnation, the person will hopefully come back as a human but may fall into one of the lower realms and have to wait thousands of years or more to have another chance at experiencing a human life. However, many Buddhists believe it takes truly heinous deeds to merit a rebirth into a lower realm, and that most people come back as humans within a short period.

The four types of enlightenment flow one to the next and are the result of successfully following the Eightfold Path and understanding the Four Noble Truths. Attaining the four enlightenments guarantees one will no longer experience lower states of being.

The four states of enlightenment are said to occur spontaneously and completely. These little enlightenments may be subtle or earth-shattering but come suddenly, and it may take time for the practitioner to realize the benefits of their achievement.

Stream-Enterer

The stream-enterer is the first level of enlightenment. These beings have fully grasped the Noble Eightfold Path and understand the importance of becoming enlightened, practicing the teachings of the Buddha, and living within a community of like-minded people. Stream-enterers fully actualize proper view and are no longer plagued by doubt or simple attachments.

Once-Returner

The once-returner is the second level of enlightenment. In addition to the achievements of the stream-enterers, they have let go of lust and hate and can see reality in its true state.

Beings who have achieved the first two stages of enlightenment no longer reincarnate as animals, hungry ghosts, or embodiments of suffering in hell. It is said that the once-returners will only come back as human one more time before becoming an *Arahant*, or awakened one.

Non-Returner

The third level is the non-returner, also called *Anagamin*. The non-returner may not be completely enlightened upon her human death, but has progressed far enough to earn the right to exist in one of the five pure abodes of higher consciousness where she will achieve enlightenment without coming back into one of the six realms of illusion. Anagamins have overcome all mortal attachment to the senses and the sensory world. Even this remarkable level of achievement is not enlightenment, however.

Awakened One

The fourth level of enlightenment is that of *Arahant*, or awakened one. It means the same thing as Buddha, but the term *Buddha* is reserved for Siddhartha Gautama, who discerned the way to enlightenment on his own. All who follow the Buddha's path and achieve enlightenment are called Arahants. Their consciousness has developed to such a degree that they see through the veil of samsara and are no longer bound by it. Arahants stop incarnating into this world of illusion, including the pure abodes. Arahants exist beyond what we know as reality.

The stages of enlightenment can occur within a single lifetime. As each level of enlightenment is experienced, afterward a Buddhist must continue their practice and their daily lives. In Zen Buddhism there is a saying: "Before enlightenment, chop wood, carry water. After enlightenment, chop wood, carry water." The body continues to exist until the natural process of death arrives.

Buddhists believe that to waste a human lifetime is tragic, as being born into a lower state of consciousness is the beginning of a long process leading to life in a human form. Once you're born as an animal, for example, Buddhists believe it may take hundreds or thousands of lifetimes to come back as a human. It may take even longer. Unlike the Western concept of heaven and hell, Buddhists do not believe in any permanent existence in any of the six realms. Ultimately we are all bound for enlightenment and all six realms of desire are illusions to be transcended.

Because Buddhism relies so heavily on individual effort, Buddhists have a strong belief that morality is imperative if one wishes to achieve enlightenment. Much moral understanding can be gleaned by studying the Noble Eightfold Path. For example, the concept of proper speech dictates that we not tell lies, that we not berate others with unkind words, and so on. Buddhists believe that only the moral can achieve enlightenment, not for a religious reason of good and bad but because moral people are calm enough within to really learn how to properly concentrate, the beginning step on the path to enlightenment. No matter how long someone meditates and studies Buddhist thought, if they are living a harmful life, no good will come of their practice. In modern parlance, Buddhists must "walk their talk," the result being inner calmness, an essential ingredient in developing deep concentration.

KARMA

Buddhists recognize that the friction of life, the endless ups and downs we all experience, is a powerful catalyst for spiritual growth. It is as if life was designed to antagonize us to feel a sense of dissatisfaction and inspire us to seek out an end to our suffering. According to Buddhists, the human realm contains the best chance for spiritual growth. We suffer, we become aware of our suffering, we desire an end to suffering, and we seek out truth and are liberated with great effort.

So what drives our life experiences? Buddhists recognize several influencers of life quality: *utu*, natural phenomena such as hurricanes; *dharma*, natural law of the universe such as motions of planets; *bija*, the quality of our genetic seed; *chitta*, the quality of the mind; and, finally, *karmaphala*, which means action and the result of action.

Karmaphala is the longer word we know as karma. *Karma* means "action" and *phala* means "fruit." In Western vernacular, karma is often misunderstood as receiving just punishment for former bad deeds, but that misses the mark. Karma simply means action. There is no Santa Claus counting up all of our good karma actions and bad karma actions and doling out consequences or rewards accordingly.

To Buddhists, karma explains the process whereby intentional actions create cause-and-effect relationships in the world of samsara, or illusion. Everything we do has an effect on the world around us. Karma can be as basic as a worrywart giving themselves an ulcer to the Buddha perfectly embodying the principles of the Eightfold Path and achieving enlightenment.

Buddha said, "It is intention that I call karma; having formed the intention, one performs acts by body, speech, and mind." These physical, verbal, and mental actions are karma. The way we think, what we say, and how we act is what creates our reality. Understanding karma helps us understand the Buddhist worldview and explains why Buddhists see reincarnation as the result of our positive or negative actions. In this sense, karma doesn't send us to any of the upper or lower realms of existence as some external force. Our own karma, our own predilection for peace or violence, spiritual insight or material existence, causes us to be attracted to one or another of the available realms of existence.

Karma is something that is sown, like a seed. Conscious meditation and other aspects of the Eightfold Path are applied to daily living and spiritual practice in order to cultivate good karma and plant the seeds of future states of consciousness. It's akin to the concept of "build it and he will come." Choosing to live the precepts of the Eightfold Path results in good life actions, with the intention that the rewards of deciding to live according to the Eightfold Path will lead to enlightenment and escape from samsara.

The concept of karma is a wonderful aspect of Buddhism for the modern world. Buddhism cultivates kind, helpful, and conscientious citizens who do not shy away from work or responsibility. Buddhism spreads a message of joy and compassion for all life and actually requires its followers to live what most religions would consider a holy, morally upright life.

But with everything going on in the world today, how can we possibly hope to remember these many facets of Buddhism and ensure we truly are actualizing them in our lives and not just in our imaginations? In the next chapter we'll explore the solution to this problem and discuss the concept of the Three Jewels of Buddhism: Buddha, Dharma, and Sangha.

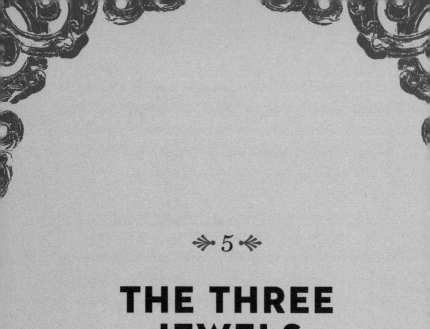

⟫ 5 ⟪

THE THREE JEWELS

BUDDHISTS EMBRACE THE CONCEPT OF THE THREE Jewels as essential because the jewels help them focus on their spiritual development. The Three Jewels are the concepts of Buddha, Dharma, and Sangha. They embody three important aspects of Buddhist teaching about the path toward enlightenment.

BUDDHA

The first of the Three Jewels is the Buddha, but this concept refers to more than just Siddhartha Gautama who became "the Buddha." The Buddha said there were many Buddhas who have lived before him and many who will follow. Therefore the concept of Buddha means anyone who has achieved enlightenment at any period in history. Many enlightened beings have become teachers to those still struggling on the spiritual path. It is considered a holy act to teach others once you've crossed the finish line yourself.

Enlightenment comes from within, and each experience of enlightenment is completely unique. Before enlightenment we benefit from those who can teach us how to deepen our understanding of the nature of reality. Honoring the role of the teacher is also embodied in the term *Buddha*.

In life, the Buddha presented himself as an example of an awakened being, one who had reached enlightenment. He was the first teaching of Buddha during his lifetime. His "Buddha nature" represents an external manifestation of a state of being available to all forms of life. Eventually all beings will become enlightened. Buddha as one of the Three Jewels represents our highest spiritual potential and the goal of our very existence.

DHARMA

The second jewel is Dharma. There is Dharma and then there is dharma. Little *d* dharma refers to the nature of reality, the transitory manifestations of reality according to natural law. Dharma in this sense refers to the teachings of the Buddha. Tradition holds that the Buddha presented eighty-four thousand teachings during his lifetime. These were first memorized, then eventually written down, and make up what is known as *Buddhadharma*. Devout Buddhists study and meditate on Buddha's teachings in order to hasten their enlightenment. Living in accordance with the teachings of the Buddha is seen as a requirement to reach enlightenment, so studying the words of the Buddha seems matter of course.

Buddhists strive to live the Dharma in a manner that assures freedom from dissatisfaction, thus leading to enlightenment. When Buddhists live a spiritual life they are said to be living their Dharma. Dharma is related to the highest ideal within your being, your inherent spiritual purpose in life. We have already learned much about the Dharma, or the teachings of the Buddha, in previous chapters on the Four Noble Truths and the Noble Eightfold Path.

In Hindu terminology, dharma can mean "duty" or "rules." A Hindu would say, "Live your dharma," as if to say fulfill your destiny but also carry out your duties in life. It could also mean "do that which you were born to do." The Buddha took this concept further when he expressed the Dharma as the embodiment of his teachings. His teachings were about the path to enlightenment, which entailed the cultivation of joyfulness, compassion, and bliss from within. Since little *d* dharma also means the world in which we live, the reality in which we exist, the combined meaning of Dharma to Buddhists can be something like, "Follow your path to freedom." In following this blissful path, Buddhists will naturally embody the principles of the Four Noble Truths, the Noble Eightfold Path, and the Three Jewels.

Since our ultimate nature is contained within, following our Dharma at its heart means becoming like the Buddha, becoming an awakened being. Finding one's Dharma is an important achievement on the spiritual path. One common way many Buddhists have found to achieve this is to live in Buddhist communities, whether isolated monasteries or gathering places in civilization.

SANGHA

Community is the third jewel and is called the Sangha. Sangha is the community of experienced or enlightened beings Buddhists seek for counsel and support on the road to spiritual awakening. Sangha also refers to any Buddhist monk or nun of any level of spiritual understanding, and in some schools of thought includes absolutely anyone who follows the teachings of the Buddha, whether Buddhist or not.

To be in the presence of experienced Buddhists is a very fortunate experience and is why special significance is given to high-level Buddhists. They are not worshipped as gurus, as one finds in the Hindu religion, but are merely respected and honored for their achievements. Many experienced Buddhists are seen to have special abilities to convey wisdom and teachings more quickly to students who are ready to receive them. The Buddha said, "Few are the people who make it to Nirvana unaided."

Taken together the Buddha, the Dharma, and a good Sangha are supposed to make it easier to reach the ultimate goal of enlightenment, but there are many stories of people who achieved enlightenment without one or more of them incorporated into their lives.

Commitment to the Three Jewels is seen as a requirement to become Buddhist. Once a Buddhist, reflection upon the meaning of Buddha, Dharma, and Sangha makes up a common meditation practice. In Buddhism, meditation is not a passive act where the mind is emptied. On the contrary, many practices require active reflection upon a particular concept. Such mental efforts are considered to be powerful allies on the path to enlightenment, as they prepare the mind to comprehend the true nature of reality and actually experience enlightenment within.

Today Sanghas exist all over the world. There are myriad schools of Buddhism, some recognized by Buddhists worldwide and others seen as local or new cults. Each of these is a type of Sangha. In the busy modern world, finding a community of Buddhists with whom you can study is a great way to learn about Buddhism. The Buddha said, "An insincere and evil friend is more to be feared than a wild beast; a wild beast may wound your body, but an evil friend will wound your mind." A Sangha of like-minded individuals help one another toward their common aim of attaining enlightenment.

The three jewels of Buddha, Dharma, and Sangha provide the structure within which a person can more easily realize their own awakening. Remember that in Buddhism there is no higher power to save you; all liberation comes from within and is the result of your own personal efforts. The concept of the Three Jewels asks us to learn from the Buddha and live compassionately—from his teachings of the Dharma to become wise, and from the Sangha to share whatever we have to offer with the world.

✦ 6 ✦

BECOMING A BUDDHIST

FOR THOSE WHO WISH TO FOLLOW THE STEPS OF the Buddha and achieve enlightenment, the requirements are very simple. Aspiring Buddhists perform the ceremony known as "taking the three refuges." Different Buddhist sects have minor variations on this ceremony, but basically a person makes a commitment to the Buddha, Dharma, and Sangha. Buddhists must also agree to follow the five precepts of not killing, stealing, or lying; not getting intoxicated (including drugs); and refraining from sexual misconduct. Make these commitments and you're an official Buddhist.

The Buddha said that in order to follow his teachings one must "Avoid all evils; do all that is good; purify one's mind." He also said that if a person can have loving-kindness while being tortured by thieves, then that person is a real follower of the Buddha. Hopefully it'll never come to that, but you get the idea: Buddhists hold wisdom and compassion as the highest expression of spirituality. Wisdom implies understanding the teachings of the Dharma, the collected works of the Buddha, rather than simply rote memorization or vapid agreement. Real efforts must be made to cultivate wisdom. Likewise, we must all express compassion as a central tenet of our lives, not because the Buddha said so, but as a natural expression of an awakened consciousness. Remember that evil is seen to be simply deep ignorance, and those who are conscious beings are incapable of performing evil deeds. Instead, such awakened Buddhists emanate joy, peace, and compassion as a matter of course.

There are millions of "armchair Buddhists" who study the Buddha's teachings, practice meditation, strive to live according to the structure of the Eightfold Path, and generally work to improve the conditions of the world. Many of these people call themselves Buddhist. Many go on intensive retreats of one sort or another and take the teachings of the Buddha very seriously. Once someone has embarked on the path of enlightenment, Buddhists believe there is no going back. Though the process of becoming enlightened may take thousands of lifetimes, eventually that spark of desire for liberation will continue to grow and that person will one day fully awaken.

Mental development is a hallmark of Buddhism. This does not mean to increase the quantity or quality of one's thoughts, but to control the endless array of random thoughts that flow through the mind. Once achieved, we more quickly proceed toward enlightenment. The Buddha once said, "To enjoy good health, to bring true happiness to one's family, to bring peace to all, one must first discipline and control one's own mind. If a man can control his mind he can find the way to Enlightenment, and all wisdom and virtue will naturally come to him." Similar Buddha sayings reveal the simplicity of his teaching.

The Buddha asked his followers to have an active practice. He asked us to bring "peace to all" and "happiness to one's family." Human relationships are normally fraught with ups and downs, and we may endure varying degrees of stress as we attempt to get along with family and friends, coworkers, and neighbors. It is just these seemingly negative conditions that provide humanity with the spiritual food necessary to sprout the inner bodhisattva seeds lying dormant within each of us. While some Buddhists think that even the monastic life is too distracting and live in a cave in a forest, there are those who relish city life. All forms of human activity give us opportunities to hone our ability to love our enemies (and friends), share what we have with the world, and spread joy and compassion by choosing to act with kindness and conscious intent.

The teachings of the Buddha recognize the power of free will to help or harm humanity. When we take the vows of the Three Jewels and become a Buddhist, we are agreeing to attempt what at first sounds impossible: to deliberately choose kindness and conscious self-awareness for the rest of our lives under any and all circumstances.

The Buddha taught these concepts five hundred years before the time of Christ. Some 2,500 years later, humanity still struggles with the same passions, self-doubt, and stresses that existed in the days of the Buddha. Many religions preach of an end time when external life events will change and bring about a more peaceful world. The end time could be the end of a cycle of time, some astrological change in the heavens, or an act of a god or goddess or other external forces. In Buddhism it all comes down to you, the individual, and you're asked to do the impossible. Buddhism describes a completely foreign type of existence, enlightenment, which must coexist back in the world from whence it came, a world that isn't even real. Buddhists seek enlightenment to understand what's really going on in the universe but also to then remain in this illusory world of samsara and help other beings awaken, too.

The path of Buddhism begins with a simple commitment to embrace compassion, be kind, study the teachings of the Buddha, and mingle with like-minded people. These are simple steps that anyone can accomplish with just a little effort. Kindness is perhaps the easiest. Kindness is integral to the life of a Buddhist. As the Buddha said, "Thousands of candles can be lighted from a single candle, and the life of the candle will not be shortened. Happiness never decreases by being shared." Living in a state of exceptional joy, kindness, and compassion is seen as a sign one walks the path of the Buddha. In the next chapter we'll learn more about the Buddhist take on love and kindness.

THE AWAKENED HEART

T HERE IS MUCH TALK OF THE MIND IN BUDDHISM, but the meaning of the word is different from what we may typically think "mind" means. It does not mean thinking, but instead the more basic idea of consciousness. In fact, the typical act of thinking, the constant flow of thoughts that race through our minds endlessly, is seen as one of the major sources of dukkha, or ignorant dissatisfaction, that plague humanity. In Buddhist terms, mind means our capacity to think and feel, whether consciously or unconsciously.

SELF VERSUS OTHERS

The awakened consciousness of the bodhisattva lies dormant within all humans. Buddhists recognize that much suffering comes from our personal desire and attachment to things in the world around us. For Buddhists, these are examples of basic human ignorance.

In contrast, Buddhists engage in selfless activities for the benefit of others. These actions are based in compassion to end all suffering in the world. Performing selfless acts on behalf of humanity fosters feelings of happiness and joy.

When we focus on our own problems, we are basically saying that the issues of one person are more important than every other living being in the entire universe. However, the wish to alleviate the suffering of all beings in the universe has the potential to touch an infinite number of lives. This subtle shift in consciousness from self to others opens our consciousness to a greater understanding of the state of the world and allows for our awareness to fill that larger world.

To exclusively focus on either the self or others is equally off balance. By bringing to our attention the idea of living our lives in such a way that we may be of service to the world, we can bring balance between our inner and outer life. As humans we have a tendency to become more focused on the self than on others; both are equally important and a balance between the two is necessary to achieve enlightenment.

Regarding the self, how should we approach satisfying our own needs? The first step in answering this question is to seek understanding about what is truly important for the self, and to which part of the self we speak of when supporting self-interest. For Buddhists the answer is very clear. The inner self that deserves attention is our inner seed of Buddhahood waiting to be nurtured and fertilized into a fully enlightened being. Therefore, focusing on the self does not mean figuring out how to honor ourselves with a new house or car, or any other mundane activity. To serious Buddhists, no earthly needs outweigh the necessity for inner spiritual growth save that of the basic survival needs of nourishment, water, and a place to sleep and meditate. No attachment is given to general worldly things. Buddhists lovingly and compassionately alter their existing lifestyles to align with the teachings of the Eightfold Path. By embodying the Eightfold Path, we awaken inner consciousness and wisdom. The needs of the self are to awaken. At the very least, spiritual awakening benefits others with compassion and service. Such an attitude minimizes the importance we give to everyday sources of stress; the worries of life become less important.

Regarding others, the end goal of an enlightened being is assisting in the enlightenment of other beings. The Dalai Lama has a wonderful saying: "Whenever possible, be kind. It is always possible to be kind." Being present to others with kindness, compassion, and even joy is transformative. Exemplifying these qualities in everyday life will never cause harm to others, and that alone is a worthy accomplishment. And the potential exists to inspire others to seek spiritual awakening as a means to find their own inner kindness, compassion, and joy, just as the Buddha felt on his trip through the city when he beheld the happy holy man.

BODDHICHITTA

The whole idea of living in a balanced way to achieve enlightenment for the benefit of all beings is called boddhichitta. *Bodhi* means "awakened," *chitta* means "heart," "mind," or "attitude," but *boddhichitta* is generally translated as "the awakened heart," meaning conscious compassion. Cultivating boddhichitta is a way for Buddhists to move toward an enlightened state of being, but developing true boddhichitta may take years of meditative training. To cultivate boddhichitta means to develop the deep wish that all beings achieve enlightenment, even if that means they all achieve it before you do. It's related to the idea of boddhisattvas or enlightened beings taking a vow to postpone the perfection of their enlightenment until all other beings can join them in an enlightened state. Boddhichitta is a desire to help others on the deepest level and requires opening our hearts to the suffering of the world and choosing love anyway.

A statement of boddhichitta can be something like, "May all beings experience true happiness and the causes of happiness; may all beings be freed of ignorance and the causes of ignorance." Boddhichitta is the way of compassion. Compassion and wisdom work together to prepare the space within for the experience of enlightenment. Wisdom without compassion is incomplete, and vice versa. The Eastern view of mind combines the Western view of mind and heart. So for the purposes of educating the Western mind about Buddhist thought, it can be said that a wise person lives from the spiritual heart, not the intellectual mind. This is why the

Buddha said, "The way is not in the sky. The way is in the heart." The way refers to the Middle Way, or the Noble Eightfold Path, often seen as a path of intellectual development and searching but in truth has more to do with transcending mental thoughts and basic emotions to reach a place where awareness arises from a place of compassion, in the West associated with the heart.

The idea of the awakened heart means wisdom married to compassion. The desire to embody boddhichitta inspires Buddhists to practice the six perfections of generosity: ethics, patience, effort, single-pointed concentration, and wisdom. For Buddhists, this type of wisdom means something more than mental understanding. Wisdom transcends the mind and is the result of direct comprehension of truth. The Buddha said, "We are shaped by our thoughts; we become what we think. When the mind is pure, joy follows like a shadow that never leaves." Active self-development with the aim of becoming a physical embodiment of joy, wisdom, and compassion for the betterment of the world is one of the many things that make Buddhism such a unique philosophy.

The cultivation of boddhichitta reminds me of another interesting aspect of Buddhism. Much like modern pop psychology, Buddhists focus on cultivating positive attributes rather than those personality traits they wish to be rid of. While other religions focus on the abolishment of sin and performing penance for one's actions, Buddhists are taught to accept their incomplete natures as a matter of course and not to attach any negative emotions or thoughts about the current state of their spiritual development. By focusing on their desired positive outcomes, Buddhists believe they will eventually grow such qualities within themselves that their basic unwholesome natures will fade into the background.

INCOMPLETE BEINGS

Buddhists incorporate positive affirmations, creative visualizations, group meditations on various positive themes, and other similar methods to cultivate a new, positive spiritual persona. They believe that human beings are born with an entirely different persona at birth. This birth persona exhibits certain characteristics that are the result of past life experiences, inherited family traits, and other social and natural phenomena. Buddhists also believe that we are all born spiritually asleep. Just as a baby isn't capable of steering its own destiny at birth, the same can be said of the Buddhist's perspective on fully grown human beings. Physically we may be all grown up but spiritually, even psychologically and emotionally, we are but simple children. Buddhists see normal everyday people as incomplete beings, seeds waiting to sprout open and become what they were meant to be. It is only through conscious effort that this new persona awakens.

Because Buddhists see ordinary humanity as incomplete, the personality cards we're dealt at birth don't matter in relation to our spiritual development. We all start at ground zero. None of us, or at least very few of us, are born remembering much about why we're here or where we came from. In each lifetime we start over and have to relearn how to awaken. From the Buddhist perspective, humanity is therefore all equal. No one is higher or more important than another by virtue of birth or social status. It is only through the attainment of spiritual awakening through diligent and consistent efforts that respect and recognition are bestowed. When asked what makes a "great man," the Buddha said, "It is by freeing the mind that someone becomes a great man. Without freeing the mind one cannot be a great man."

So how does boddhichitta relate to our awakening, to freeing our minds? The Buddha considered every human being to have a connection with boddhichitta. Boddhichitta represents a part of us that is already enlightened. Therefore, living in boddhichitta indicates one is on the path to enlightenment. Buddhists recognize boddhichitta as a force that anyone can tap into even during their darkest hours. Anyone at any time, no matter their level of spiritual awakening, can choose to love and feel compassion over another's suffering. Existing in a state of compassion and loving-kindness helps us spiritually awaken.

Exercise: Loving-Kindness Meditation

The following meditation can be performed whenever you have an extra fifteen minutes to spare. There are many variations of this practice, both in words and length of practice. The intention is what's most important. With continued practice, this meditation will shift from a mere repetition to feelings of hope, happiness, and compassion. This meditation involves repeating certain words over and over. Think of them as positive affirmations or intentions for your life.

Begin by finding a comfortable place to relax and meditate. Take several deep breaths and allow your mind, emotions, and body to calm and relax. When you feel ready, repeat the following words internally for roughly fifteen minutes.

"I am filled with loving-kindness. I am well. I am peaceful. I am happy." While you repeat these words over and over, visualize yourself being held by loving-kindness. During this meditation curl your mouth slightly into a gentle smile. A gentle smile has a powerful psychological effect and will help you feel well, peaceful, and happy.

Repeat this meditation as often as possible for several months, always smiling and always focusing on the self. An expanded practice of this meditation is, after meditating for you, to add loving-kindness for others, eventually holding intention of loving-kindness for the entire world, the entire universe. But first things first: Begin by trying to remain focused enough to shower yourself with loving-kindness for fifteen minutes several times a week. The Buddha reminds us that "You can search throughout the entire universe for someone who is more deserving of your love and affection than you are yourself, and that person will not be found: You yourself, as much as anybody in the entire universe, deserve your love and affection."

8

DEATH, TIME, AND NOW

THE CONSCIOUS PREPARATION FOR DEATH IS another fascinating aspect of Buddhist philosophy. The Buddha taught that our entire reality is an illusion from which we must awaken. Time and space don't really exist; they are constructs of our group imagination. However, the illusion is so strong, so perfectly manifest, that we are deeply trapped within it and believe it to be real. In the eyes of the Buddha, the illusionary world in which we live is so compelling that we become inextricably attached to every passing phenomena, lifetime after lifetime. We attach to external objects and people that don't really exist as they appear to us; we become attached to the endless variety of inner states that grab our attention, from joy to sorrow.

Not surprisingly, after the Buddha came to the realization that we're living in a dream, he wanted to wake up. He placed great emphasis on waking up from the illusion within a single lifetime.

Not a moment could be spared. Whereas Hindus were restricted from meditation and other spiritual practices except for within prescribed religious boundaries, the Buddha taught that everyone should practice at every possible opportunity, whether meditating, eating, or even sleeping. Achieving self-awareness, self-awakening, and enlightenment can be seen as a race against time because our lives are so short. The great Buddhist goal is to spiritually wake up before our consciousness experiences death and is forced to rebirth in another body in another lifetime. Buddhists believe that we forget all of our past life experiences and connections at the moment before birth and intense efforts to reawaken must start all over again.

In the West we don't talk much about death, and even less so about what happens after death. Even those with religious beliefs leave it up to their chosen higher power to decide their postmortem fates. We hear stories about people having near-death experiences, including white light, the appearance of departed loved ones, or visions of heaven or hell. While many individuals do believe in some sort of afterlife, mass media portrays these stories as mere vivid imagination. For Buddhists, however, death is the subject of much study and meditation and is given much respect. Death is seen as the great motivator of spiritual effort because its approach is guaranteed, and it comes nearer each day of our lives.

To emphasize the importance of time and the inevitability of death, Buddhists engage in two types of meditative practices, one external and one internal. Externally, Buddhists may visit cemeteries, attend funerals, and otherwise spend time coming face to face with the inherent mortality of the human body. Accepting death helps Buddhists make the most of their short human lifespans. Since death comes closer every day, Buddhists believe there is no time to waste. All available time must be devoted to self-awakening. This may conjure images of saffron-robed Buddhists meditating from dawn until dusk, but for thousands of years many Buddhists have been ordinary citizens raising families, working hard, and handling their daily responsibilities. Such people are termed *good householders*. While fulfilling their life duties, these people engage in regular Buddhist spiritual practices and do their best to live the Noble Eightfold Path. There are many stories of ordinary people, nonmonks, who achieved enlightenment.

Internally, Buddhists prepare themselves for death by performing special meditations that involve visualizing the death process. In the Western world, this is most well known through the writing of Tibetan Buddhists. In *The Tibetan Book of Living and Dying*, author Sogyal Rinpoche provides the West with an illuminating glimpse into some of the spiritual practices Tibetan Buddhists perform to prepare for death. These special practices help Buddhists visualize the many stages of consciousness experienced during death. By engaging in these "dry runs" of the death process, Buddhists hope to acclimate themselves to the spiritual sights and sounds occurring during death. Buddhists believe that after death we are flooded with all manner of images, sounds, memories, smells, and other sensations. The intense sensations mimic the intensity of the world we live in right now and seem just as real, though they are just as false. If we aren't prepared, we will be pulled into our next incarnation in part by whatever sensation we're most drawn to. Buddhists hope to prepare themselves to resist the many images they'll experience after death and instead remain focused on what is called the clear light of consciousness.

Tibetan Buddhists also meditate upon the death process to eliminate the fear of death. Fearlessness toward death allows experienced Buddhists to successfully maneuver through the wild sensations experienced at death and allow them to reincarnate in the most desirable way possible, if at all. Buddhists believe it possible to successfully detach from sensory visions and consciously choose a next birth or even choose to not come back at all. Buddhists believe it is possible to achieve enlightenment during the death process.

THE ETERNAL PRESENT

A benefit of mindfulness meditation, or self-observation, is it fosters a heightened sense of presence. The Buddha said, "Do not dwell in the past, do not dream of the future, concentrate the mind on the present moment." Buddhists value the ability to live completely aware in the present moment for many reasons. Living fully present diminishes attachments, increases single-pointed concentration, keeps the body and mind calm, and minimizes random thoughts. But Buddhists also believe that beyond time and space exists the eternal present.

The eternal present is difficult to explain from the perspective of the world in which we live where time marches on and the universe expands infinitely around us. If life is an ocean of movement, the eternal now is a single drop of water. The drop holds everything within itself, unmoving and unchanging. The Buddha taught his students about an entirely different reality than the one we're born into. Through the realization of our impending death, the Buddha hoped to inspire his followers to begin the process of awakening immediately. The great benefit of meditation is that it brings awareness into the present moment. Consistent meditation also increases our ability to concentrate. Concentrating in the present moment is seen by Buddhists to have great benefit toward our spiritual awakening, in part because it helps us remain clear and calm and focused during the death process.

Most people go through life pulled along and distracted by life duties, inner affectations, and insecurities. But death is coming. Every day death comes closer. There is nothing we can do about this situation. If we do not have the ability to stay calm and present, to remain focused and concentrate in this lifetime, then Buddhists see little hope of increasing any of these skills upon death. This would be like expecting to ace an exam without any knowledge of the subject matter, or waiting to learn how to swim until you're swept away by rising floodwaters. Buddhists see the human experience as the beginning of another form of consciousness, Nirvana, but unless efforts are made to start the process of awakening right now, our consciousness is endlessly recycled from body to body, life to life.

Death is seen as a very turbulent experience. First of all, death itself is a major shock to consciousness. Suddenly consciousness exists without a body, without the world we were born into. Rich imagery, intense sounds and smells, and memories of all types come rushing into our awareness. Buddhists believe many people experience the death and rebirth process scared out of their wits. Others attach to loved ones, unfulfilled dreams, or negative emotions about past deeds or missed opportunities. All of these things are attachments to the dream of life, to samsara, and Buddhist practices aim to transcend all of this unnecessary suffering by developing single-pointed concentration and heightened awareness. It is only through spiritually waking up that we are able to see through the illusions presented to us in life and in death and perceive what is really happening.

The goal of Buddhists is to awaken completely, rise above the wheel of karma, and thus break the cycle of reincarnation. Meditating upon death reminds Buddhists to practice; engaging in specific death meditations trains Buddhists to prepare for the death process and not be distracted from Buddha consciousness, the consciousness of enlightenment. In this way, liberation is achieved. The belief in the unending cycle of rebirth into one of six illusory worlds is so strong that it forms the one and only goal of existence: to wake up enough to stop being pulled back into the illusion of life. The Buddha affirmed that it is possible to awaken in a single lifetime at any moment, even during death. Buddhists believe there is much to be done to prepare for death because even if we become enlightened during our lifetime, we must still live out the remainder of our lives. All humans eventually go through the death process; therefore Buddhists prepare constantly for their transition from this life to the next.

The idea of cultivating awareness about your impending death all the time may seem a bit morbid, but you can't deny that death is a great motivator. In the modern world there seems to be an obsession with youth culture. Mass media programs us to appear, act, and live as eternally youthful. Modern knowledge of the human body has increased the average lifespan as well as the quality of life for many older adults, yet death is always there, waiting at the end of life with open arms. For a Buddhist to miss achieving at least the lower levels of spiritual awakening in this lifetime means that that person will definitely have to reincarnate, hopefully as a human but perhaps as something else. Remember that Buddhists believe in six worlds where beings of all types live out their lives. No matter which world Buddhists live in, they believe that being reborn means forgetting everything that came before and starting over from scratch. Maybe they'll be reborn into a life conducive for renewed spiritual growth but perhaps not. To put all effort toward awakening in this lifetime is all Buddhists can control. Life is a race against time and inevitable death, where we'll have to experience the *bardo* of becoming all over again, or the state of consciousness we experience before our consciousness precipitates into its next lifetime.

THE SIX BARDOS

Tibetan Buddhists break human consciousness down into six states, or six bardos. The word *bardo* can be translated as a "transitional consciousness." Each bardo has unique properties and represents a different aspect of the human experience. Buddhists believe one bardo dissolves into another. Some bardos overlap, while others exist as isolated states of consciousness. Originally the bardo meant only the fifth bardo listed below, the bardo of becoming, but over time other aspects of the cycle of living and dying have been realized.

The First Bardo

The first bardo is the consciousness of birth and living out our lives until our very last breath. In other words, the bardo we're living in right now. While in the first bardo we may also experience the second and third bardos.

The Second Bardo

The second bardo is the consciousness of our dreams. Tibetan Buddhists see dreaming as another great opportunity to prepare for life after death. There are many practices whose aim is the development of waking-quality consciousness while in the dream state. Tibetan Buddhist Tenzin Wangyal Rinpoche is a popular writer on the subject of conscious dreaming. Dreams are illusions that pull us along their story arc in a similar way that waking consciousness does. As Rinpoche writes, "If we cannot carry our practice into sleep, if we lose ourselves every night, what chance do we have to be aware when death comes?" Again we see the idea that the reality we experience now is merely an opportunity to prepare for what is to come after death.

The Third Bardo

The third bardo is consciousness during meditation, or samadhi. Meditation is a state of self-recognition and is a crucial aspect of Buddhist philosophy that will be covered more in depth in the next chapter. Buddhists engage in active meditations to increase awareness of their inner and outer worlds. The goal of meditation is to develop an ever-present awareness undistracted by inner or outer states. When distractions arise, they do not break the attention and our awareness remains clear. For those who have practiced correctly, it is possible to remain in the state of samadhi during the process of death. Buddhists see such an achievement as being very beneficial and allowing for the possibility of enlightenment upon death.

The Fourth Bardo

The fourth bardo is consciousness at the moment of death. Buddhists believe in five forces, or elements, that allow consciousness to exist in this world. They are the four elements of earth, water, fire, and air and the fifth element of space. The five elements correspond with the living experiences of weight or mass, fluidity, temperature, movement, and open space within which we exist. Buddhists believe that when the five elements are in balance so are our lives. When they're out of balance, we become sick. This explanation is extremely simplified but describes the basic philosophy of the five elements. Upon death the five elements dissolve and what it means to feel human disappears. Such a loss is a shock to our consciousness and can lead to much confusion during the death process. An unprepared consciousness usually means an overdeveloped ego, or attachment, to the life that just expired. Since most people's identity aligns with their physical appearance, once the body is gone and only consciousness remains there can be much sadness, anger, and confusion over the sudden change. Conversely, Buddhists who have practiced diligently, cultivated joy and compassion, lived the Noble Eightfold Path, and developed single-pointed concentration through meditation do not experience much suffering during the dissolution of the five elements because their level of attachment to the body is already low.

Buddhists firmly believe it is possible to maintain complete awareness during the death process and recognize the five stages of dissolution as they occur while remaining calm and serene. In addition, Buddhists believe many advanced practitioners meditate for several days after their death in a state of heightened samadhi. However, normally the trauma of death plunges us into unconsciousness for a period. We black out for several "days" before reawakening into the fifth bardo.

The Fifth Bardo

The fifth bardo is consciousness experiencing its own nature and the nature of reality. This is the bardo of becoming, for our experiences here shape our next lifetime. For most people the fifth bardo is full of seemingly real and very distracting images, sounds, smells, and other projections of their own consciousness. The quality of the projections is based on the quality of the previous life. For those who have prepared themselves and received much of clear light consciousness, the fifth bardo flashes past as if watching a TV show. In other words, the experience is observed from a detached point of view and has no effect on the consciousness. For those caught up in their passions, likes, and dislikes, the fifth bardo sets the stage for the quality of their next rebirth. During the fifth bardo, people often attempt contact with loved ones, visit places of strong attachment, and experience other strong attachments from the previous life. Eventually acceptance of death occurs and the rebirth process begins. In the fifth bardo people may experience all of their belief systems, attachments, hopes, and dreams all at once. Visions of heaven or hell, positive and negative fantasies of all kinds, beguiling images of long-lost loves, and other distractions can easily absorb the attention.

Advanced Buddhists may experience clear light consciousness, which is ever present during the fifth bardo. Experiencing clear light depends on the level of awakening achieved during the previous lifetime. If one remains detached to their own mental manifestations, one may recognize the clear light all around them. In very beneficial instances, the realization of the clear light leads to instant enlightenment and the cycle of death and rebirth breaks.

The Sixth Bardo

The sixth bardo is the consciousness of rebirth into a new lifetime. Again, those who achieved some manner of awakening in a previous life, not enough to enlighten but enough to experience clear light consciousness for a period, remain alert during the process of rebirth, while those caught up in their attachments experience more karmically induced visions. Either way, at the moment of rebirth, or the return to the first bardo with the first inhalation of breath, the wave of forgetfulness washes over us and all memory of the intermediate bardo, as well as all previous cycles of life, is gone.

The Buddha cautioned that "Thinking habits can harden into character. So watch your thoughts." In relation to the teachings on the bardo, the quality of our previous lives that causes a positive or negative rebirth is based upon the greater or lesser degree of attachment we've cultivated in that previous life. Unhealthy attachments to food or drink, drugs, sex, violence, the ego, pride, vanity, and other negative traits are believed to cause us to reimagine such things during the final bardo of becoming. The Buddha's warning is not so much a moral one as a practical one. Do not be moral to avoid an after-death judgment; do it to cultivate thoughts and actions that minimize reattachment to this world. For this world doesn't really exist. Buddhists strive to live a moral life in order to manifest higher and higher rebirths and eventually achieve enlightenment. It's easy to see why this type of morality is not based on a desire to impress a god or goddess with their great deeds; living a life of high morality is a means to an end. Buddhists believe the bardo of becoming, the fifth bardo, can really mess up an otherwise pleasant experience. Death may come as a shock, but the clear light experience of the fifth bardo, loosely akin to descriptions of heaven, is seen as a positive experience. The fifth bardo is also believed to be an opportunity to spontaneously wake up into enlightenment. When a prepared consciousness is exposed to clear light consciousness, there's a chance for intense spiritual awakening. Instead of going through the cycle of rebirth, a person chooses to follow the pure light instead.

Tibetan Buddhist teachings are very complicated and full of specific rituals. As with the rest of this book, the concepts expressed here are just the tip of the iceberg. Refer to the recommended reading list at the end of this book for more thorough investigations into Buddhist concepts and literature on such complicated subjects.

Now that we've been introduced to the concept of the six bardos, let's look more at the third bardo, the practice of meditation.

⇥ 9 ⇤

MEDITATION

ALMOST EVERYONE HAS HEARD OF MEDITATING, and meditation is recognized internationally as a wonderful way to reduce stress and relax. Meditation is defined as an exercise leading to contemplation. Many cultures have unique meditation methods and define meditation differently. In this chapter we will explore how Buddhists define meditation, examples of meditation as spiritual practice, and some basic meditation techniques.

The Buddha had much to say about meditation as a helpful tool on the path to enlightenment. He explained many meditation methods and techniques and, in particular, highlighted two benefits of meditation that made the practice worthwhile to those seeking enlightenment. Those benefits are achieving serenity of mind and developing personal wisdom.

Buddhists consider everyday humanity to be as if asleep, ignorant of the true nature of reality. So how do we go about waking to an enlightened state of consciousness? The Buddha said, "Oh monks, if the four foundations of mindfulness are practiced persistently and repeatedly, the seven factors of enlightenment will be automatically and fully developed." Let's explore, then, the four foundations of mindfulness that automatically lead to the seven factors, or types, of enlightenment. Indeed, the seven factors of enlightenment are an aspect of the fourth foundation.

FOUR FOUNDATIONS OF MINDFULNESS

Satipatthana, or the four foundations of mindfulness, is an important part of Buddhist practice. The collection of teachings and exercises contained within the four foundations help Buddhists gain insight into the nature of reality and themselves. Mindful awareness such as self-observation is the key to enlightenment. Buddhists believe we only spiritually awaken, or become mindful, with great effort. The four foundations of mindfulness can also be interpreted as the four foundations of awareness. The four foundations of mindfulness are the mindfulness of the body, feelings, mind, and mental manifestations. A famous discourse by the Buddha, called the Satipatthana Sutta, explains the Buddha's teaching on the four foundations as follows:

This is the only way, monks, for the purification of beings, for the overcoming of sorrow and lamentation, for the destruction of suffering and grief, for reaching the right path, for the attainment of Nirvana, namely, the four foundations of mindfulness. What are the four?

Herein a monk lives contemplating the body in the body, ardent, clearly comprehending and mindful, having overcome, in this world, covetousness and grief; he lives contemplating feelings in feelings, ardent, clearly comprehending and mindful, having overcome, in this world, covetousness and grief; he lives contemplating consciousness in consciousness, ardent, clearly comprehending and mindful, having overcome, in this world, covetousness and grief; he lives contemplating mental objects in mental objects, ardent, clearly comprehending and mindful, having overcome, in this world, covetousness and grief.

1: Kayanupassana: Mindfulness of the Body

The first practice is mindfulness of the body. To cultivate awareness of the body, Buddhists have developed six practices, as follows:

ANAPANASATI: BREATHING

Mindfulness of breathing is a common introductory practice for developing awareness, and it is the same as the exercise described at the end of Chapter 3. Mindfulness breathing is typically a sitting meditation where one focuses on the in-breath and the out-breath, though there are many variations of the practice. The idea is to become grounded and fully present in this illusory world from within your own center. Buddhists sit in a comfortable position and remain seated for long periods simply focused on the breathing. The mind reminds us of so many different things that suddenly need doing—errands, new projects, old projects, family duty, millions of endless things. But we must continue to sit and be present. Thoughts come and go, smoke and fog on the mirrors of our consciousness, but our awareness remains and we sit. Breathe in, breathe out. This practice is believed to develop self-discipline. Breath awareness is the foundation upon which future practices can be built.

IRIYAPATHA: BODY AWARENESS

Mindfulness of the body is more active than the previous exercise and involves remaining aware of the body at all times, whether sitting, standing, moving around, or lying down. As with breath focus, the goal here is simply cultivating awareness. Thoughts come and go, restlessness ebbs and flows, distractions abound, but we simply remain aware of the body in a nonjudgmental way. We become more present in our experience of being in a body.

SATISAMPAJANNA: CLEAR COMPREHENSION

Mindfulness of clear comprehension helps develop the beginnings of true wisdom and discernment by living in full awareness. Basically, throughout our day, whether getting ready for the day, watching TV, or doing any other activity, we bring our inner awareness to observe the day unfold while cultivating an awareness of the purpose, suitability, presence, and understanding of our actions. We become mindful of our way of being in the world: when we're present or not, when we act with purpose or not, when we act in harmony with the Eightfold Path or not, all nonjudgmentally.

KAYAGATASATI: REFLECTION ON THE REALITY OF THE BODY

Reflection on the reality of the body is designed to help us better understand that we are not our bodies. Human bodies are made up of many parts that come together as a living form. Buddhists list thirty-two parts of the body. This practice is more commonly known as "reflection on the repulsiveness of the body" and is thought to aid in the elimination of attachment to lust. Even though the Buddha advised his students to care for the body since it houses our consciousness, we must learn to give up the belief that we are our body. When we die the body is no more; only our awareness remains.

DHATUVAVATTHANA: MATERIAL ELEMENTS OF THE BODY

Again, as an aid to minimize attachments to the body and its functions, Buddhists reflect upon the four elements that make up the physical body: earth, air, fire, and water. In this sense, the word *elements* is used as an idea or concept and not as a literal description. Each element has many characteristics, such as earth being associated with the body, water with emotions, and so on. Developing awareness of the elements of the body helps us detach from feeling ownership of experiences caused by one or another element.

SIVATHIKA: CEMETERY REFLECTIONS

As mentioned in the last chapter, to bring awareness to the belief that we are not our bodies, Buddhists incorporated meditations at a cemetery into their spiritual practice. Buddhists believe that one of the greatest illusions plaguing humanity is the false hope of immortality. We all believe there will be time to do x or y activity someday in the future, when in reality time is extremely short for all people and action must be taken now. Buddhists strive to drive that point into their consciousness by reflecting upon dead bodies, cemeteries, and anything else that brings awareness to their mortality.

2: Vedananupassana: Contemplation on the Feelings

The second foundation of mindfulness is called contemplation of the feelings. In Buddhism the feelings are general experiences of reality instead of emotions like happiness or fear. The Buddha talked about three groups of feelings: pleasant, neutral, or unpleasant; bodily or mental; and worldly or unworldly. Cultivating awareness of feelings helps us understand our inner motivations, levels of attachment or detachment from sensory life, as well as the transient nature of life. Buddhists believe it is only our attachment to illusory reality, to samsara, that keeps us all here. Becoming aware of attachments, our feelings about things, can ultimately lead to our detachment from them. Therefore, we move into a position to choose if we want to come back into the illusion of life or not.

3: Cittanupassana: Awareness of the Mind

Similar to the previous practices, the third foundation of mindfulness, awareness of the mind, seeks to help Buddhists increase awareness of illusory reality to help overcome attachment to it. In this case the attachment is to the mind, or the level and quality of consciousness. Practitioners become aware of thought motivations and understand their basic level of consciousness. In other words, Buddhists learn what their thoughts revolve around. It may be lust, anger, jealousy, or any number of random distractions. On the other hand, the mind may be full of love, peace, and compassion, and be clear from right understanding of the nature of things.

Humans tend to observe others instead of themselves. Mindfulness practices help bring awareness back to the self, not to boost the ego but to shred it to bits. Becoming aware of who we really are deep down can be a humbling but necessary experience, especially if we aim to progress correctly on the path to enlightenment and not continue being deluded by life.

4: Dhammanupassana: Contemplation of Mind Objects

The fourth foundation of mindfulness is becoming aware of the many things our minds attach to that create the circumstances for our continual involvement in the endless cycle of death and rebirth. As we've seen throughout this book, Buddhists are fond of grouping things together, and mental objects are no exception. Buddhists believe by bringing awareness to the following groupings, we begin to free ourselves of their influences over our lives. With much dedication and practice, Buddhists believe it is possible to awaken a true conscious awareness that observes and interacts with our illusory reality in a clear and conscious way. Those who have developed these qualities are held in high regard by Buddhists because success comes only after much effort. Now we will briefly look at the many groupings of mind objects.

NIVARANA: FIVE HINDRANCES

The five hindrances refer to the primary distractions in our daily lives that keep us bound to samsaric attachment in this dream world. The five are lust, anger, laziness, worry, and doubt. To counter the five hindrances Buddhists identified five antidotes, as follows. Body meditation or single-pointed concentration (reflecting upon the temporary nature of our lives) is used to overcome lust, or attachment to other bodies; loving-kindness or rapturous bliss for anger; activity and active meditations for laziness; breath awareness for stress; and study for doubt.

KHANDHA: FIVE GROUPS OF EXISTENCE

The five groups of existence represent those things we cling to as our ego or personality. They are materiality, feelings, perceptions, mental creations, and consciousness. Remember that Buddhists believe that our entire reality is an illusion, a creation of mind. The illusion includes our bodies, attachments and feelings, the things we choose or do not choose to see, our imaginations about the world, and our ego sense of self. All of these things are part of the megadream we call reality. Bringing awareness to the five groups of existence helps us realize we are not our body, we are not our thoughts, etc. There is something observing reality unfolding, and this something else is our true nature.

AYATANA: TWELVE FOUNDATIONS OF MIND

The twelve foundations of all mental activity are those aspects of existence that encourage us to believe this world we're living in is real. When any of the twelve activities are activated by the way we engage with the world around us, we also perpetuate the illusion. Unconscious engagement in the world leads to unhealthy attachment and therefore continual entrapment in the wheel of karmic rebirth. Remember that karma means action, and if all of our actions focus on attaching to external experiences, whether a loved one, a particular activity, or even a way of looking at the world, then we always will choose to come back into the illusion, rebirth after rebirth. The twelve foundations of the mind are the six senses and the things that stimulate that sense. They are eye and form, ear and sound, nose and smell, tongue and taste, body and touch, consciousness and idea or imagination. The twelve foundations of mind are one of the Five Aggregates in Chapter 2.

SAMYOJANA: TEN FETTERS

The next grouping of mind objects is the ten fetters, which, as the name implies, are ten things Buddhists believe tie living beings to the endless wheel of death and rebirth. The ten fetters are: believing in a personality, skeptical doubting, attaching to rules and rituals, sensuous craving, focusing on ill will, craving for abundance, craving for immaterial existence, being conceited, feeling restless, and being ignorant. Buddhists believe that becoming free of the first three fetters means you are definitely on your way to enlightenment. Those who have overcome the fourth and fifth fetters are called once-returners, meaning they'll only come back as a human one more time. Those who achieve more than this are non-returners, at least to earth. And those who have freed themselves from all ten fetters are basically enlightened ones, or Arahants. You may remember we looked at the once-returners, non-returners, and Arahants earlier in this book. Buddhist concepts are looked at from many angles in many ways, and there are several practices available for each concept.

BOJJHANGA: SEVEN CAUSES OF ENLIGHTENMENT

The final collection of mind objects is the seven causes of enlightenment. These are mindfulness, investigation, courageous effort, joy, calm, concentration, and equanimity. As the last of the four foundations of mindfulness, the seven causes of enlightenment begin with mindfulness. Unless mindfulness has been achieved, there is no ability to truly perceive reality for the illusion that it is.

With mindfulness, Buddhists can clearly investigate the true nature of phenomena. Buddhists do not mean a scientific investigation of researching a hypothesis and analyzing the results of a study. Instead, investigation is more similar to intuitive insight where realization comes all at once. Awakening consciousness is applied to the nature of existence, and reality is observed and understood from a place beyond thought and thinking, at least when the second cause of enlightenment, investigation, is fully actualized. Truth is simply perceived.

The third cause, courageous effort, refers to the energy spent maintaining a focused awareness that is directly engaged in conscious observation of reality, both internally and externally. This type of effort has been described as unending patience in the face of great adversity. It corresponds to right effort on the Noble Eightfold Path.

Happiness, joyfulness, and rapture are the characteristics of the fourth cause of enlightenment. Many times the Buddha said there can be no enlightenment without joy. There are no unhappy spiritual masters. All have found peace and joy within. As with the Buddha's statement that enlightenment must come from our own efforts, Buddhists believe the same about happiness. There is no outer cause for happiness. We either choose to be happy or not—the choice is ours alone to make.

The fifth cause of enlightenment is calmness or tranquility of body and mind. All fidgetiness of the body and mind has ceased. Without calm, it is impossible to fully concentrate. The idea here is that our consciousness is born into a machine called the human body that allows us to experience an imaginary world, what we call reality. Through intense efforts, we are able not only to wake up within our machine body but also to control it properly. Since the goal of Buddhists is waking up, all other endeavors take second stage. Wandering imaginations, tapping a beat with the feet to a favorite piece of music, or any other fickle expressions are seen as indications of an unfocused mind. Again, since life in a body is an opportunity to prepare for death, Buddhists believe that developing tranquility will help us be able to concentrate during the intensity of the death process.

The previous five causes of enlightenment move forward into the sixth cause, concentration. All the previous accomplishments allow the development of one-point concentration where truth can be discerned for what it really is. The five hindrances previously described have been completely transcended and are no longer distractions on the spiritual path. All desire for sensual things has passed. All anger, ill-will, stubbornness, laziness, restlessness, worry, and doubt have vanished.

Combining all the previous causes of enlightenment leads to the seventh, the state of equanimity, where one remains calm in the face of life's many ups and downs, twists and turns. Buddhists who have reached this state of being remain fully present in all situations, and no matter how involved they become in a particular situation, their inner state remains one of detachment and compassion.

SACCA: FOUR NOBLE TRUTHS

Buddhists include the Four Noble Truths, which also includes the Noble Eightfold Path, in the four foundations of mindfulness as a reminder that it is necessary to fully understand the Four Noble Truths in order to gain enlightenment. Buddhists see their philosophy as an interconnected series of ideas and practices that work together to help them spiritually awaken.

In these very structured teachings of the Buddha, which are further broken down into myriad subdivisions, the Buddha laid out a specific series of steps to take to achieve enlightenment. Buddhism can be explained as a type of scientific spirituality, similar to the science of psychology, where scientists realize that emotions exist even though they cannot always be controlled or even measured physically. The Buddha took all of his experiences and, in a tediously methodical manner, described exactly how he had achieved the state of consciousness he called Nirvana. This book merely scratches the surface of this detailed system of knowledge laid out by the Buddha. Some aspects of spiritual development are broken down into finite minutiae and can sometimes become a hindrance to the foundational teachings he presented that make up the chapters contained in this book.

Another way the Buddha described his path of spiritual refinement was his teachings on the eight jhanas, or "states of meditative concentration." Legend has it that the Buddha had two primary teachers and that these teachers originally taught him the eight jhanas. The first seven he learned from Alara Kalama. The eighth he learned from Uddaka. Feeling that these teachings did not help him answer the questions of how to transcend old age, death, and sickness, the Buddha left these teachers and headed out into the wilderness to continue his spiritual practices alone. During this time, he realized what some Buddhists call the ninth jhana.

THE EIGHT JHANAS

The jhanas, also called dhyanas, are states of meditative concentration. Their development relates to right concentration on the Noble Eightfold Path, as the first four jhanas are seen as expressions of right concentration. Similar to mindfulness meditations that focus on the breath, practice of the jhanas uses the same technique to develop a oneness of consciousness that includes the subject and the object at the same time. This is difficult to describe until one has experienced the sensation, and many advanced Buddhist practices unfold under the guidance of a more experienced Buddhist who can recognize the signs of advanced development in their students.

Buddhists describe the experience of the jhanas as transformative, and they caution that their intensity can be confused with achieving enlightenment. Even though the jhanas are steps along the way to enlightenment, they are important steps nonetheless. At higher levels of attainment, the jhanas are associated with the development of special abilities that correspond to the Western concept of extrasensory or psychic traits. Such traits are seen as naturally occurring phenomena that must be kept under the strictest control. Buddhists do not encourage the use of such powers if they manifest as a result of spiritual practices because they may give unhealthy boosts to the ego, which may cause increased attachment to the world of illusion in which we live. Therefore, although it is believed to be an inevitable result of advanced Buddhist practices, psychic abilities are never used in public.

To experience the jhanas, it is said that students must be practicing good morality as defined by the Noble Eightfold Path as proper speech, action, and livelihood. Without sufficient morality, there is too much attachment, craving, and desire for worldly things. It is only when a student is ready to give up the things of the world that an opening in their consciousness occurs that allows the experience of the jhanas to occur. And remember that morality means nothing like a Christian morality of punishment and reward. Morality is a means to an end, the end being detachment from the material world.

Let's take a look at the eight jhanic states of being and how they are experienced by Buddhists. The first four states deal with physical sensations and are called fine-material jhanas, and the second four with spiritual experiences and are called immaterial jhanas.

Fine-Material Jhanas

After many hours, months, years, or decades of meditation, Buddhists may achieve the first jhana, described as the onset of happiness and joy as a result of long periods of undisturbed single-pointed concentration on a particular subject, typically the breath, but it could be anything. Once the level of concentration is highly refined, one is able to remain concentrated on the subject (breath, symbol, etc.) while shifting the attention to the spontaneous onset of joy.

PLEASANT SENSATIONS

A unique aspect of the jhanas is that all pain disappears at the onset of the jhanas. It is common for meditators to feel uncomfortable and endure long willful battles between the mind's desire to avoid discomfort and the meditator's resolve to remain concentrated and unmoving, before the onset of the first jhana. It is ironic how Buddhists, in an attempt to wake up from this world of illusion and suffering, put themselves in physically uncomfortable situations for hours on end.

The light at the end of the tunnel is the onset of the jhanas, the first of which is enough to dispel all painful sensations. The joyful bliss that is felt can reach such intensities as to feel ecstatic in the religious sense of the word. The body hums with pleasure as the levels of joy increase. This jhana can therefore be a very distracting experience.

JOY

To progress from the first to the second jhana, the practitioner must remain aloof to the sensations and not become attached to entering the jhanas simply to feel joyful or pleasurable feelings. While a remarkable achievement, there is much that follows. Buddhists who can remain dispassionate to the physical sensations of joy, bliss, and rapture and instead focus on the emotional state have reached the second jhana. The feeling of concentration should deepen and the feeling of calm should deepen, even as the rapturous experience of bliss pours from the heart.

CONTENTMENT

Remaining still unmoved by any of these joyful sensations, Buddhists who eventually enter the third jhana experience a contentedness that is more satisfying than the brilliant throes of bliss and joy that affected the body and emotions before. The intensity of contentment increases the ability to remain detached from the sensory experiences of the world. Contentment also enhances the quality of compassion. In essence, the third jhana is reached by getting used to the intense feelings of joy and rapture and realizing that they are just sensations like anger or happiness, though much more intense.

Releasing attachment to sensations allows the student to feel the calmness and contentment underneath the pizzazz of rapture. Rapture happens, but life goes on.

COMPLETE PEACE

Contentment can become a hindrance as well. Buddhists who remain ever calm and centered, even toward the sensation of contentment, reach the fourth jhana. This state of being is neither this nor that, content nor discontent, joyful nor miserable. All that remains is the focus of the spiritual mind and the feeling of utter peace. There are no more sensations.

To even describe such a state of being as desirable for an otherwise living being may seem odd from the perspective of ordinary existence. It may seem logical to learn methods to avoid feeling or experiencing the negative aspects of humanity such as anger, fear, or stress, but why would someone wish to detach from the positive experiences of life, like joy and bliss? Remember that Buddhists believe that there is a reality separate from the dream we're currently living in, and that this world is a much better place. To be attached to anything in our world is to succumb to the possibility of its opposite. To attach to joy inevitably leads to pain when the joy ends, however temporarily. The Buddha discovered a place outside of such oppositional experiences and spent the rest of his life trying to explain to those who would listen exactly how he reached the new reality, Nirvana. To experience Nirvana, all attachment to the experiences of our everyday world must be recognized for the dreamlike state they are.

Immaterial Jhanas

The transition from the fourth jhana of peace beyond sensation to the fifth jhana occurs when the meditator, existing in a state of consciousness without form, shifts their awareness to the boundaries of their being, as if watching the self from afar.

INFINITE SPACE

Awareness of the physical form is replaced by awareness of the boundaries of space. The meditator's awareness fills the room, as if filling the building, neighborhood, planet, solar system, and galaxy, out into boundless space. The idea of space in this jhana is more than the physical idea of space and doesn't mean that a meditator will literally fill all space, although the inner sense is of quite literally feeling infinite space.

Imagine the shock of going from the boundaries of our physical body to the vast infinity of space. The first experience of this jhana is just as jolting as the feeling of total rapture experienced earlier.

INFINITE AWARENESS

The sixth jhana is achieved by the realization that there is a consciousness observing all of that infinite space, and then shifting the attention to that consciousness. The realization is that consciousness exists beyond time and space. At each level, consciousness, concentration, and the process of awakening reaches new heights, new levels of completion.

Despite the amazing experience described in this jhana, there is still more. Buddhists of this degree feel at one with all existence but are not yet enlightened. There is still a connection to the world of space and time, and this state of being has been confused with a oneness with all existence.

EMPTINESS

The seventh jhana requires moving beyond the experience of consciousness to perceive that which comprises consciousness, which is emptiness. Those who experience the seventh jhana become aware that everything held within consciousness is ultimately without any lasting quality to give it a permanent nature. The dynamic of the universe is change, physically and spiritually. Every aspect of reality is in motion and manifests in ever new and changing ways.

The realization of emptiness lays bare all attachments as meaningless. If nothing is real, then there is nothing to be attached to. Even so, the recognition on such a deep level that there is no permanent reality, there is no you, me, planet, galaxy, universe, time, history, or future, is not enough. There is more awakening to do.

BEING, NEITHER PERCEIVED NOR IMPERCEIVED

Those who achieve the eighth jhana have let go still further and enter a quirky state of consciousness full of things that "are" and "are not" at the same time. Buddhists at this level release the perception of infinite space and experience a deep inner place of calm. The utter sense of calm is unbreakable. The eighth jhana could be described as in the world but not of it. Consciousness is aware of the happenings of daily life but by and large exists outside of space and time. Mind as we understand it is not present in this state. There is no naming of things by the mind, no this and that, yet awareness is still present in the world of "this" and "that." The eighth jhana is pure consciousness.

Such an abstract concept is difficult for us to grasp from our current state of being, embroiled as we are in the highs and lows of life, the necessary duties and obligations that we all feel so compelled to follow. Pulling back the curtain on what we call reality is deeply transformative and is best experienced rather than described.

This is as far as the Buddha reached during his studies with Alara Kalama and Uddaka before entering the forest to continue his studies alone.

There is some debate as to the ultimate benefit of the development of the jhanas. Some schools of Buddhism see them as essential to breaking free of the bonds of ignorance that keep us endlessly recycling from death through rebirth. Others see the fantastical experiences of the jhanas and the associated psychic powers, or siddhis, that result from their development as major hindrances on the path to enlightenment. The important point is to remember to remain dispassionate and detached from whatever is experienced during the jhanas. They are of benefit to the development of deep, focused concentration, loving-kindness, and compassion. Some argue that the experiences of the jhanas don't spill over into nonmeditative periods, whereas other meditative methods such as vipassana breathing practices, which involve active meditations on the changing nature of reality, allow for the development of permanent and lasting higher awareness. This perspective comes from the previous quote from the Buddha that if a person maintains constant awareness for seven days they will become enlightened.

THE NINTH JHANA: CESSATION

What the Buddha discovered beyond the eighth jhana is fairly incomprehensible from our current state of being. The Buddha describes another level of being and that he was not alone in this place. He described his accomplishment as having rediscovered something that had been previously known on earth in times as ancient to him as the Buddha is to us, perhaps much earlier. From a passerby's perspective, the Buddha, in the state of the ninth jhana, would appear comatose or asleep, barely breathing, barely moving, barely thinking, barely doing anything we would consider as awake, and yet his awareness was greater than it had ever been.

There is some debate surrounding the idea of the ninth jhana, if something beyond the eight jhana is actually vipassana meditation, or if what the Buddha achieved was something else entirely. As described here, the ninth jhana means a state of being beyond the human experience, beyond a personal point of view. Some Buddhists believe that liberation occurs upon reaching the experience of cessation of feeling and perception, while others say that enlightenment is reached at a state beyond even this rare achievement.

✦ 10 ✦

THE PATH OF PEACE

A LITTLE BIT OF BUDDHA HAS ONLY SCRATCHED the surface of Buddhist philosophy, but the teachings contained within these pages comprise the foundation of most Buddhist schools. Beyond this introduction to Buddhism are multiple layers of teachings, commentaries, and subcommentaries.

Many aspects of Buddhist practice are best pursued under the careful guidance of a more advanced Buddhist. Dissolving attachments is a major undertaking and leads to many unexpected situations. Some Buddhist schools are more esoteric, while others strive to incorporate Buddhist philosophy into the fabric of local culture. An example of this is how aspects of Tibetan Buddhism have been influenced by the native Bon tradition.

Buddhism is the path of peace. Buddhists are well known for their peaceful words and deeds. If nothing else, Buddhist meditation can lead to a lasting sense of calm and inner peace that is hard to criticize. And since Buddhism is a philosophy and not a religion, there are many people who take up Buddhist practices while still following the dictates of a chosen organized spiritual doctrine.

Since the morality of Buddhism is aimed at the eradication of karma and the severing of attachments of all kinds, living peacefully is an inherent part of Buddhist culture. Any immoral or unkind word or deed is believed to have rippling effects that tie us down to the cycle of death and rebirth. As the Buddha said, "Hatred is never appeased by hatred. Hatred is only appeased by love. This is an eternal law."

Minimizing attachments to the everyday world may seem to lessen the highs of life, its joys and triumphs. However, more importantly, this practice diminishes life's lows. Sorrow, fear, anger, and a lack of compassion create a world without lasting peace. As Buddhists embrace their spiritual practices, they counteract those experiences and contribute to a more peaceful society.

Because Buddhism assumes a world in which there is no higher power, its teachings possess a sense of urgency. You must choose to be happy. You must choose to be mindful. You must choose to be peaceful and you must choose to spiritually awaken. For some this path is difficult; for others it's like coming home, a practice filled with great joy.

Buddhism is a nonjudgmental philosophy in that it accepts all people's incomplete natures as a necessary truth. It is only through personal effort that we can be made whole and wake up from within.

Living peacefully is necessary for this awakening to occur. But this requirement of peace isn't demanded blindly. Peace is a natural expression of growth on the path of Buddhism: Those who awaken become peaceful. Through rigorous meditative practices contained in Buddhist teachings, followers learn to see through the veil of samsara, the dream-illusion we call reality in which we live. In this way, Buddhists learn the truth of suffering and discontent as well as how to liberate themselves from suffering. Buddhism's long spiritual journey leads to a place of intense peace and calm.

The journey to peace is a hallmark of Buddhism and one reason Buddhism has become such a popular philosophy to practice. In the busy modern world, more and more people seek inner peace. Buddhism's amazingly rich trove of wisdom offers a straightforward path to peace for people of every level of spiritual development. The next section, Additional Resources, lists several popular books on Buddhist philosophy from several different Buddhist schools of thought that will help you begin your own journey—or continue on the path that you have already chosen to follow.

ADDITIONAL RESOURCES

For more information about Buddhism, the following resources are a wonderful place to begin. Much of the general information about Buddhism and quotes by the Buddha in this book were referenced from these works.

Catherine, Shaila. *Wisdom Wide and Deep: A Practical Handbook for Mastering Jhana and Vipassana*. Somerville, MA: Wisdom Publications, 2011.

Chödrön, Pema. *Awakening Loving-Kindness*, abridged. Boston: Shambhala Pocket Classics, 1996.

Dalai Lama, His Holiness the. *How to See Yourself as You Really Are*. New York: Atria Books, 2006.

Evans-Wentz, W. Y. *Tibet's Great Yogi Milarepa: A Biography from the Tibetan*. London: Oxford University Press, 1928.

Fronsdal, Gil. *The Dhammapada: Teachings of the Buddha*. Boston: Shambhala, 2008.

Hagen, Steve. *Buddhism Plain and Simple: The Practice of Being Aware, Right Now, Every Day*. New York: Broadway Books, 1997.

Hanh, Thich Nhat. *The Heart of the Buddha's Teaching: Transforming Suffering into Peace, Joy, and Liberation*. New York: Broadway Books, 1998.

Irons, Edward A. *Encyclopedia of Buddhism*. Edited by J. Gordon Melton. New York: Checkmark Books, 2008.

Osho. *The Buddha Said . . . : Meeting the Challenge of Life's Difficulties*. London: Watkins Publishing, 2007.

Padmasambhava. *The Tibetan Book of the Dead*. Edited by Graham Coleman and Thupten Jinpa. New York: Viking Penguin, 2006.

Powers, John. *Introduction to Tibetan Buddhism*, rev. ed. Ithaca, NY: Snow Lion Publications, 2007.

Rinpoche, Anyen. *The Union of Dzogchen and Bodhichitta*. Ithaca, NY: Snow Lion Publications, 2006.

Rinpoche, Sogyal. *The Tibetan Book of Living and Dying*. San Francisco: Harper San Francisco, 1992.

Rinpoche, Tenzin Wangyal. *Awakening the Sacred Body*. New York: Hay House, 2011.

———. *The Tibetan Yogas of Dream and Sleep*. Ithaca, NY: Snow Lion Publications, 1998.

Salzberg, Sharon. *Loving-Kindness: The Revolutionary Art of Happiness*, rev. ed. Boston: Shambhala, 2002.

Schmidt, Amy. *Dipa Ma: The Life and Legacy of a Buddhist Master*. New York: Blue Bridge Books, 2005.

Snyder, Stephen. *Practicing the Jhanas*. Boston: Shambhala, 2009.

Suzuki, Daisetz Teitaro. *An Introduction to Zen Buddhism*. New York: Grove Press, 1994.

Trungpa, Chogyam. *Shambhala: The Sacred Path of the Warrior*. Boston & London: Shambhala, 1988.

———. *Cutting Through Spiritual Materialism*. Boston: Shambhala, 1973.

ENDNOTES

Introduction

"Today there are well over": Pew Research Center's Forum on Religion & Public Life. "The Global Religious Landscape." December 2012.

Chapter 1

"Historians agree he was an": Powers, John. *Introduction to Tibetan Buddhism*, rev. ed. Ithaca, NY: Snow Lion Publications, 2007.

"The oldest surviving Buddhist texts": Roseth, Bob. "The Bark of the Buddha." University of Washington alumni publication, 1997.

"There are too many to": Buswell, Robert. *Encyclopedia of Buddhism*. New York: Macmillan Library Reference, 2013; Irons, Edward A. *Encyclopedia of Buddhism*. Edited by J. Gordon Melton. New York: Checkmark Books, 2008.

Chapter 2

"It is only by making": Suzuki, Daisetz. *The Lankavatara Sutra: A Mahayana Text*. Motilal Banarsidass, 2009.

"The words used are *tanha*": Rahula, Walpola. *What the Buddha Taught*. New York: Grove Press, 1974.

"In contrast, the final craving": Morrison, Robert. "Three Cheers for Tanha." *Western Buddhist Review*, vol. 2. http://www.westernbuddhistreview.com/vol2/tanha.html.

"Despite the doom and gloom": Thera, Nyanaponika, Natasha Jackson, C. F. Knight, and L. R. Oates. "Mudita: The Buddha's Teaching on Unselfish Joy." Access to Insight. 8 June 2010. http://www.accesstoinsight.org/lib/authors/various/wheel170.html.

Chapter 3

"The word normally translated to": Sanskrit Dictionary for Spoken Sanskrit. spokensanskrit.de.

"Therefore, most schools of Buddhist": Bodhi, Bhikku. "The Noble Eightfold Path: The Way to the End of Suffering." *The Wheel Publication*. no. 308–311. Sri Lanka: Buddhist Publication Society, 2006.

"Even early Buddhists were advised": Brahmavamso, Ajahn. "What the Buddha Said About Eating Meat." Newsletter, Buddhist Society of Western Australia, April–June 1990.

"The Buddha said, 'Mindfulness of'": Bhikku, Thanissaro. *Maha-satipatthana Sutta: The Great Frames of Reference*. Burma Pitaka Association, 2000.

Chapter 5

"The Three Jewels are the": Mizuno, Kogen. *Essentials of Buddhism: Basic Terminology of Buddhist Philosophy and Practice*. Tokyo: Kosei, 1996 (reprint).

"They embody three important aspects": Sangharakshita. *The Three Jewels: An Introduction to Buddhism*. London: Rider, 1967.

Chapter 6

"Make these commitments and you're": Rinpoche, Sakyong Mipham. "Becoming a Buddhist." *Shambhala Sun*, September 2000.

Chapter 7

"Boddhichitta is a desire to": Rinpoche, Anyen. *The Union of Dzogchen and Bodhichitta*. Ithaca, NY: Snow Lion Publications, 2006.

Chapter 9

"'Herein a monk lives contemplating'": Analayo. *Satipatthana: The Direct Path to Realization*. Windhorse Publications, 2004; Thera, Soma. *The Way of Mindfulness: The Satipatthana Sutta and Its Commentary*. Buddhist Publication Society; 5th ed., 1941.

INDEX